"Michael Tompkins has gathered the best of what works into a straightforward, no-nonsense guide that will help readers to understand why they are anxious and to develop a step-by-step plan to beat anxiety. People with a range of anxiety-related problems—from panic attacks to obsessive-compulsive disorder to phobias—will get tremendous benefit from this insightful, compassionate, and practical book."

—**David F. Tolin, PhD, ABPP**, author of *Face Your Fears*

"In this user-friendly book, Tompkins helps the reader use scientifically proven strategies to overcome problems with anxiety. Readers will learn about how anxiety problems function, how to select appropriate treatment targets, and how to implement cognitive-behavioral strategies—the most effective interventions for getting out of the anxiety cycle. Complete with lots of worksheets and illustrative examples from beginning to end, this book is a must for sufferers and therapists alike."

—**Jonathan S. Abramowitz, PhD**, professor and associate chair of psychology, University of North Carolina at Chapel Hill

"In *Anxiety and Avoidance*, Tompkins describes tools and concepts for overcoming anxiety that are based on the latest scientific developments in the field, and on his many years of clinical experience working with adults, teens, and children suffering from anxiety's debilitating effects. Tompkins' deep understanding of anxiety and its effective treatment shines through on every page.

> —**Jacqueline B. Persons, PhD**, director of the San Francisco Bay Area Center for Cognitive Therapy and clinical professor in the Department of Psychology at the University of California, Berkeley

"*Anxiety and Avoidance* is an excellent guide for anyone who is anxious. Filled with self-help forms and useful tools, readers can readily find relief by following this guide. Highly recommended."

> —**Robert L. Leahy, PhD**, director of the American Institute for Cognitive Therapy, New York, and distinguished founding fellow and diplomate of the Academy of Cognitive Therapy

"Many of us have a tendency to avoid people and situations we find unpleasant and/or emotions and bodily sensations we find distressing. These habits of avoidance can inadvertently create many problems for us, contributing to negative vicious cycles, including escalations in anxiety and fluctuations in our mood. This incredible and most practical book helps us all to develop healthier habits and overcome avoidance, improve our motivation and more clearly identify our goals and values. By using the skills Tompkins provides, we can step out of the small box that many of us live in and enjoy living the biggest and fullest versions of our lives."

> —**Allison G. Harvey, PhD**, professor of psychology and director of The Golden Bear Sleep and Mood Research Clinic, University of California

"Tompkins has made a significant contribution to the anxiety self-help literature. His work integrates elements from several established cognitive and behavioral therapies and appropriately reflects the field's growing emphasis on producing a single, unified approach to all anxiety disorders. Most importantly, Tompkins has translated complex terms and concepts into a language that can be readily grasped by consumers. Individuals with a variety of disabling fears should benefit greatly from this user-friendly resource."

> —**C. Alec Pollard, PhD**, director at the Center for OCD and Anxiety-Related Disorders, Saint Louis Behavioral Medicine Institute, and professor of family and community medicine, Saint Louis University

"Tompkins does it again! This is a wonderful book that explains the antecedents of anxiety in clear, straightforward terms, and then walks the reader, step-by-step, through a series of exercises aimed at treating it. The exercises and worksheets are appropriate for all types of anxiety symptoms, and can be personalized to fit almost any situation. I will recommend it to all of my clients who struggle with anxiety."

> —**Carol A. Mathews, MD**, director at the Obsessive Compulsive Disorders Clinic and co-director of the Anxiety Disorder Clinic in the department of psychiatry, University of California, San Francisco

"Research consistently shows that cognitive behavioral therapy (CBT) is highly effective in the treatment of anxiety disorders. With the sensibility of an experienced clinician and the clarity of an excellent writer, Tompkins has distilled the wisdom of multiple CBT perspectives. *Anxiety and Avoidance* provides therapists and patients with a single resource that integrates empirically validated CBT treatments. *Anxiety and Avoidance* synthesizes practical and proven strategies and provides step-by-step instructions to lead a life less impacted by fear, apprehension, and worry."

> —**Dennis Greenberger, PhD**, coauthor of *Mind Over Mood*

"I wholeheartedly recommend this book to everyone who experiences anxiety, panic, and fear to the extent that it has a detrimental impact on their lives. Experienced psychologist Tompkins has synthesized various approaches in an easy-to-read book, designed to help those with anxiety learn important strategies to overcome avoidance and feel more comfortable in anxious situations. In a compassionate style, he shows how to deal with the heart of the problem and how to maintain positive changes in the long term."

> —**Nikolaos Kazantzis, PhD**, founder and director of the Cognitive Behavior Therapy Research Unit at La Trobe University, Australia

"This book provides a refreshingly modern perspective on anxiety, panic, and fears. Packed with valuable exercises and drawing on strategies from three evidence-based therapies, the book provides readers with a variety of tools to address their difficulties in a more effective way."

> —**James Bennett-Levy**, associate professor at the University of Sydney; coeditor of the *Oxford Guide to Behavioral Experiments in Cognitive Therapy* and *Oxford Guide to Low Intensity CBT Interventions*; and coauthor of the *Oxford Guide to Imagery in Cognitive Therapy*

Anxiety and Avoidance

A Universal Treatment *for* Anxiety, Panic, and Fear

Michael A. Tompkins, PhD

New Harbinger Publications, Inc.

Publisher's Note

This publication is designed to provide accurate and authoritative information in regard to the subject matter covered. It is sold with the understanding that the publisher is not engaged in rendering psychological, financial, legal, or other professional services. If expert assistance or counseling is needed, the services of a competent professional should be sought.

Acquired by Melissa Kirk; Cover design by Amy Shoup; Edited by Nelda Street; Text design by Michele Waters

Library of Congress Cataloging-in-Publication Data

Tompkins, Michael A.
  Anxiety and avoidance : a universal treatment for anxiety, panic, and fear / Michael A. Tompkins, PhD.
    pages cm
  Summary: "In Anxiety and Avoidance, psychologist and anxiety disorder expert Michael A. Tompkins presents a universal, transdianostic approach for helping readers cope with anxiety, panic, and fear using cognitive behavioral therapy (CBT) and mindfulness treatments. This book includes mindfulness strategies, motivational tips, and cognitive tools for reframing anxiety and fear so readers can get back to living their lives"-- Provided by publisher.
  Includes bibliographical references.
  ISBN 978-1-60882-669-8 (pbk.) -- ISBN 978-1-60882-670-4 (pdf e-book) (print) -- ISBN 978-1-60882-671-1 (epub) (print) 1. Anxiety--Treatment. 2. Panic disorders--Treatment. 3. Cognitive therapy. I. Title.
  RC531.T66 2013
  616.85'22--dc23
                          2013012297

Printed in the United States of America

15 14 13   10 9 8 7 6 5 4 3 2 1   First printing

For Francie and Lori

Contents

Acknowledgments

First, I thank my wife, Luann L. DeVoss, and our daughters, Madeleine and Olivia, for their unwavering support of another book project. It is impossible to imagine doing this without them by my side.

I thank my colleagues at the San Francisco Bay Area Center for Cognitive Therapy, beginning with Jacqueline B. Persons, director, for her continued support of this book and my other books that she has nurtured along the way. I thank my other colleagues from the Center (Joan Davidson, Polina Eidelman, Janie Hong, Daniela Owen, and Daniel Weiner) for their continued support of my professional development.

I thank my editor at New Harbinger Publications, Melissa Kirk, for her steady guidance throughout the process of writing this book and for her tolerance of my missteps along the way. I look forward to our working together on other projects in the future. I thank Jess Beebe, Nicola Skidmore, and Angela Autry Gorden, also of New Harbinger Publications, for improving the quality of the book in general. I extend a special thanks to Catharine Meyers and Matt McKay of New Harbinger Publications, who provided me another opportunity to write a book with this terrific publisher.

Finally, I wish to acknowledge those who have taught me the most about helping people with anxiety disorders: people who suffer with the problem, and the family members and friends who love them. Your courage and determination to better your situations continues to inspire me and enrich my life. Thank you.

Introduction

Flexibility is the hallmark of mental and emotional health. The goal of this book is to enhance the flexibility of your thinking, attending, and acting. You'll learn to shift more easily out of your anxiety and avoidance and into more-reasonable and less-anxiety-evoking thoughts and attitudes so that you can see things as they really are. You'll also learn to shift your attention by unhooking from your anxious thoughts and anxious body, and from the objects and events in your environment that frighten you, through focusing on what you're doing here and now. You'll discover the value of stepping toward, rather than away from, discomfort, and through this process, you'll grow more confident that you can handle your anxious response and the objects and situations linked to it. Last, you'll learn to stop the senseless and frustrating anxious actions, such as checking or seeking reassurance, that you know make little sense but that seem impossible to stop doing.

As your thinking, attending, and acting become more flexible, your emotional system will become more flexible too. You'll find that it's easier to calm yourself: to shift your anxious response down when it makes sense to do this, and to shift your emotional system into high gear when that makes sense. Emotional flexibility, then, is the key to recovery from your anxiety disorder.

This book is for anyone who struggles with anxiety and for psychotherapists who are seeking a single, effective approach to help clients recover from such problems, regardless of the severity of the anxiety or, if there's a diagnosis, the specific type of anxiety disorder. The book rests on the assumption that all anxiety disorders share common factors that maintain anxiety and avoidance and that any effective treatment must target those common factors by teaching common skills. Even though this book often addresses the reader as having an anxiety disorder, if you don't have an anxiety disorder but struggle with periods of intense anxiety, the strategies in this book can help you too.

WHY A SINGLE TREATMENT FOR ANXIETY DISORDERS?

Currently, there are twelve anxiety-disorder diagnoses and over twenty-five subtypes and categories of these disorders, and we have specific treatments for about half of them. Research has demonstrated that these treatments, particularly cognitive behavioral treatments (Hofmann and Smits 2008; Norton and Price 2007), help most people recover from anxiety disorders. Over the last few years, however, researchers have been examining the effectiveness of general, rather than specific, treatments for anxiety disorders. These new treatments target core factors thought to maintain anxiety disorders in general (Erickson 2003).

There are several advantages to using a single treatment for anxiety disorders. First, many people have anxiety symptoms that don't quite meet the full criteria for a particular anxiety disorder. For example, someone might have features of social phobia and obsessive-compulsive disorder, but not enough symptoms to meet the criteria for one over the other. Often, psychotherapists diagnose these individuals with *anxiety disorder not otherwise specified* (NOS). At this time, we don't have a specific treatment for anxiety disorder NOS, nor do we know how many people have this diagnosis. A treatment that targets common factors in all anxiety disorders might help those with anxiety disorder NOS too. Furthermore, a single treatment that targets the central factors thought to be responsible for excessive anxiety and fearfulness might improve the lives of people who do not have an anxiety disorder but would like strategies to manage the excessive anxiety they experience from time to time.

Second, more than half of people with one anxiety disorder have another anxiety disorder too (Brown et al. 2001). These people must seek specific treatment for each disorder, one at a time. For example, if you have both social phobia and panic disorder, you might first receive treatment for panic disorder, followed by treatment for social phobia, or vice versa. Thus, you must delay treatment of one of your anxiety disorders until you have recovered from the other. A single treatment that targets common factors and teaches common skills might help people recover more quickly without the need to complete multiple treatments in sequence. This can save them time, money, and suffering.

Third, research suggests that the factors that are common to anxiety disorders might be common to other emotional disorders, such as depressive disorders, as well (Fairholme et al. 2010). For example, nearly half of the people who have a major depressive episode in their lifetimes also have an anxiety disorder (Regier et al. 1998). Therefore, people who have both an anxiety disorder and a depressive disorder might benefit from a single treatment that targets the common factors that contribute to both of these conditions. Furthermore, even people with an anxiety disorder who are not depressed might learn skills that will help them recover from or manage their depression if they become depressed later in life.

COMMON FACTORS AND COMMON SKILLS

The final reason why a single treatment for anxiety disorders makes sense—apart from simplifying your life and the lives of psychotherapists—is that there appears to be considerable overlap among the active components of treatments for different anxiety disorders (Norton 2006). Most treatments include strategies to increase your awareness of your anxious experience and the parts of your anxious response that contribute to it. Most treatments include ways to change your anxious thoughts and to decrease your avoidance of your anxious response and the situations and objects linked to it. Finally, most treatments include strategies to decrease the frequency of your anxiety-driven behaviors, such as checking or reassurance seeking, and to increase your willingness to practice the skills in this book, including stepping toward, rather than away from, discomfort. Because all these treatments help, researchers suggest that these common skills or strategies might tap into factors found in all anxiety disorders. A single treatment that more directly targets the essential factors that maintain problematic anxiety and avoidance might benefit more people and appears to work at least as well as specific cognitive behavioral treatments (McEvoy, Nathan, and Norton 2009), which are the psychological treatments of choice for anxiety disorders.

The skills and strategies in this book will help you change the way you experience and follow up on your anxious responses. As you'll learn in chapter 1 ("Anxiety, Avoidance, and Anxiety Disorders"), it's your response to your anxious experience that creates problems for you, not the anxious experience itself.

Increase awareness and understanding of your anxious response. Two key factors that maintain anxiety disorders are experiential avoidance and rumination. *Experiential avoidance* is your attempt to avoid your anxious response. Because you avoid your anxious response, you know less about it than you think you do. You likely are unaware of the thoughts, actions, and physical feelings that are part of it. Through increasing your awareness and understanding of your anxious response, particularly in the immediate situation in which you feel anxious, you'll develop the ability to evaluate whether or not you're truly in danger and to more accurately assess the level of threat, if any, that you're facing. Furthermore, as you become more aware of the aspects of your anxious response, you'll discover that you're better able to tolerate the experience. This will help you resist your anxious actions and increase your willingness to face what makes you anxious or uncomfortable.

Rumination is the mental process of repetitively focusing on the symptoms of your distress and the possible causes and consequences. During anxious rumination, you dwell on the threat and on how you hope to avert the disaster, solve the problem, or correct the mistakes you fear you've made. As you learn to ruminate less, you'll be better able to rise above this rigid pattern of thinking to see things as they truly are. As you ruminate less, your mind will clear and your body will relax. Learning to break free from rumination involves breaking free from a rigid pattern of thinking that has trapped you for years in your anxious response.

Nonjudgmental, present-focused awareness (watching and waiting) of your anxious response is a key skill that will help decrease your experiential avoidance and rumination. Through watching and waiting, you'll become aware of your anxious response without labeling or judging it. This will counteract your tendency to suppress or avoid your anxious response, which only makes it worse. You'll learn to "actively do nothing," because there's no real reason to do anything. Because anxious rumination focuses on the future, nonjudgmental watching and waiting in the present—also known as "mindfulness"—reduces ruminative thinking. It's difficult to focus on the "what ifs" of the future when you are focused on the present instead. Through watching and waiting, you recognize the secondary judgments that you place on your anxious response. For example, you might think, *I'm really an idiot for feeling anxious in this situation.* Such secondary judgments only make things worse. You feel not only anxious, but also guilty, ashamed, or depressed, and then you try to avoid these emotions the same way you avoid your anxious response. Learning to watch in a nonjudgmental way will give such thoughts less power and will free you to think more clearly about yourself and the situation in which you feel anxious.

Correct cognitive misappraisals that maintain your anxious response. The tendency to interpret things in particular, inflexible ways—*cognitive misappraisal*—is another key factor that maintains anxiety disorders. For example, people with anxiety disorders tend to overestimate both the likelihood that bad things will happen and the impact that bad things might have on them, if they were to happen. This is the anxious mind in action, and when you fall into this pattern of thinking and have trouble shifting out of it, you likely spend more time feeling anxious than you would like. Therefore, a primary goal in recovering from your anxiety disorder is to develop more-flexible thinking; that is, to learn to shift out of this pattern of anxious thinking when you wish, thereby decreasing your anxiety and avoidance. As you understand more about the unhelpful way in which you interpret events and situations, you'll have more influence over your anxious response. As you learn to question the accuracy of your initial assumptions and conclusions, you'll become a more flexible thinker who can consider different ways to respond to an anxiety-evoking event. Most important, as you become a more flexible thinker, you'll see that you can act differently. You'll become more willing to tolerate anxiety and step toward, rather than away from, the things that make you anxious.

Decrease anxious actions that maintain your anxious response. Another key factor that maintains your anxiety disorder is *response persistence*: the rigid ways in which you decrease your anxious response when some event, object, or situation triggers it. Checking locks or doors repeatedly because you fear someone will break into your home, asking others repeatedly to reassure you that you're not ill, and sticking to "safe" topics because you're worried that you might say the wrong thing are examples of anxious actions. These anxiety-driven behaviors—anxious actions—temporarily decrease your anxiety, which then makes it harder for you to resist doing them when you feel anxious again. Soon, these anxious actions become second nature, and you find it harder and harder to resist doing them. Furthermore, the more you do them, the less tolerance you have to feeling even low levels of anxiety. Anxious actions also make it difficult for you to learn that you're not in real danger, even when you think you are. For example, you can't learn that people will not harshly criticize you for your preferences or opinions if you never share them with others. As you learn the skills in this book, you'll find it easier to resist the pull of your anxious actions.

Decrease avoidance of your anxious response. In addition to engaging in anxious actions, which you do after an object or event has already triggered your anxiety, you might also avoid triggering the anxious response, which is another example of response persistence. You're stuck in a behavioral rut in which you act in the same anxious way—escape or avoid—even when it doesn't work. Avoiding eye contact with people, avoiding traveling far from home, and procrastinating are all examples of ways that people with anxiety disorders avoid triggering their anxious responses. To recover from your anxiety disorder, it's essential that you enhance your tolerance of your anxious response. When you're confident that you can handle your anxious response, even when your anxiety is quite high, you won't go out of your way to avoid triggering it. Typically, it's the tendency to avoid your anxious response that makes life hard for you—not the anxious response itself. The "stepping toward discomfort" skills will help with this.

Increase your willingness to approach discomfort. Another key factor that maintains your anxiety disorder is that you are less willing to step *toward* discomfort than are people without an anxiety disorder (Campbell-Sills et al. 2006; Salters-Pedneault, Tull, and Roemer 2004). Facing your fears and remaining in situations that make you anxious is not easy. Several of the skills you'll learn in this book, including nonjudgmental, present-focused awareness and changing the way you interpret events, will increase your willingness to approach what you fear and to resist the anxious actions that you use to decrease your anxiety. In addition, true willingness rests on the desire to connect with what is truly important to you. As you let your values lead the way, you'll keep your recovery on track, because you'll remember the real reason why you're working to recover from your anxiety disorder in the first place.

HOW TO USE THIS BOOK

The strategies in this book, which you'll learn in chapters 2 through 7, target the principal factors that experts believe maintain anxiety disorders. Read and complete the exercises in these chapters in the order in which they appear. This is your path to recovering from the excessive anxiety and avoidance that have made it difficult for you to live a full and meaningful life. What you learn in one chapter will prepare you for the next chapter, and as you proceed, one step at a time, you'll begin to believe that recovery is within your grasp.

In chapter 1 ("Anxiety, Avoidance, and Anxiety Disorders"), you'll learn the parts of your anxious response and how this natural and normal emotional response, over time, can develop into an anxiety disorder.

Chapter 2 ("Watching and Learning") will teach you the importance of identifying what triggers your anxious responses (the antecedents) and what happens afterward (the consequences). It's particularly important that you understand the consequences of your anxious responses, because they're likely the reasons why you decided to work toward overcoming your anxiety and avoidance.

In chapter 3 ("Moving Forward"), you'll learn ways to increase your willingness to move forward with your recovery from anxiety and avoidance. Although you can recover from your anxiety disorder, the path ahead is not easy. Moving forward will take considerable motivation and hard work on your part. You'll learn two strategies to help you keep moving forward: examining the pluses and minuses of change, and connecting with your core personal values.

Chapter 4 ("Watching and Waiting") will teach you to watch your anxious response in a different way. Watching and waiting is an essential skill to help you manage your anxious responses. In this chapter, you'll learn several strategies to help you watch and wait, including ways to anchor yourself in the present, the heart of watching and waiting.

In chapter 5 ("Thinking Inside and Outside the Anxiety Box"), you'll learn more about your pattern of anxious thinking, particularly the way you interpret and focus on situations that make you anxious and keep you trapped in the anxiety box. You'll learn strategies to step outside your anxiety box whenever you wish so that you can live a more comfortable and fuller life. Through these strategies, you'll learn to become a more flexible thinker, which will open your world and free you from the rigid pattern of thinking and acting that has limited your life.

Chapter 6 ("Stepping toward Discomfort") will show you the benefits of stepping toward, rather than away from, the situations and events that evoke your anxiety. In this chapter, you'll learn a systematic approach to overcoming the avoidance that's a central feature of any anxiety disorder. Through these strategies, you'll become more comfortable with not only the situations that make you anxious, but also the physical sensations that make you anxious and contribute to your desire to avoid a great many things.

In chapter 7 ("Keeping Going"), you'll learn to keep your recovery going. In this chapter, you'll learn the important features of a recovery attitude and develop a plan to help you resist the pull to fall back into old patterns of thinking and acting. You'll then begin to practice your plan as you finish the book.

The final chapters will cover other key elements in your plan to recover from your anxiety disorder: medications and healthy habits. In chapter 8 ("Medications for Anxiety"), you'll learn about the medications you might be taking for your anxiety disorder and, if you're not taking medications, whether it makes sense to include medication in your recovery plan. Chapter 9 ("Healthy Habits") will show you the role of regular exercise, good nutrition, and adequate sleep in recovering from your anxiety disorder.

Although the strategies you'll learn in this book are important, the overarching goal is for you to use them to cultivate a new and more effective attitude toward your anxiety and fearfulness. As you practice the skills and observe that your anxiety and avoidance decrease, you'll begin to see the benefits of thinking and acting differently. Working to become a more flexible thinker is the key to overcoming your anxiety and avoidance and recovering from your anxiety disorder. As you become a more flexible thinker, you'll be better able to raise your head above the fog of anxiety and fearfulness that has trapped you, in order to see the world as it really is—a safer place than you think.

SEE YOUR PHYSICIAN FIRST

Everyone experiences symptoms of anxiety from time to time. You might feel tense or light-headed from worrying that you might not complete a big work project. You might feel nauseous due to the stress of changing jobs or moving to a new city. However, if in the morning, your heart races and it's difficult for you to catch your breath, are these symptoms of anxiety, or do they indicate that something is wrong with your heart or lungs? If you shake, tremble, and feel dizzy several times each day, are these the symptoms of anxiety or of hypoglycemia (low blood sugar)? Many medical illnesses have symptoms that are easily confused with the symptoms of an anxiety disorder. Cardiovascular disorders, such as *postural*, or *orthostatic*, *hypotension*, can cause you to feel dizzy. Arrhythmia is a condition in which your heart skips beats or beats irregularly. Asthma or bronchitis can cause shortness of breath, and neurological disorders, such as temporal lobe epilepsy, can cause you to feel out of sorts and experience blurred or distorted vision. Medications and drugs can also create anxiety-like symptoms. Excessive caffeine or alcohol can cause you to feel anxious and panicky.

If you have an anxiety disorder, it's very likely that your physical complaints are due to the anxiety disorder, not a medical illness. In fact, it's very likely that you've already spoken to your physician about your anxiety symptoms or disorder. However, if you have not done so, before you start working through this book, tell your physician about your anxiety and request that she rule out medical conditions that might be confused with the symptoms of an anxiety disorder. Your physician will conduct a thorough medical examination and might recommend that you meet with another medical specialist for further evaluation. Follow through with such recommendations until you and your physician are confident that your symptoms are due to your anxiety alone, not a medical problem.

IF YOU'RE TAKING MEDICATIONS

People who have anxiety disorders often take medications to help manage their anxiety and avoidance. If you're already taking anxiety medications, you can continue doing so while using this book. However, taking certain medications (see chapter 8), such as Xanax (alprazolam) or Klonopin (clonazepam), every day can dampen your anxious response so that you don't get the full benefit of the strategies in this book, particularly when you're learning to step toward discomfort (chapter 6). But, unless your physician recommends it, don't change your medication or dosage while working through this book. If you must change your medication, postpone working through the book until you reach a stable therapeutic dose, and then start the book again. It's better to keep your medication the same while working through the book in order to benefit fully from the strategies you'll learn at this stage of your recovery. In addition, if you change your medication while working through the book, you might not know what is helping more: medication or your hard work.

Finally, as you work through this book, if you begin to use more than your usual amount of medication, particularly if you're taking more benzodiazepine medication than usual, this might signal that you require more support. Alert your prescribing physician that you're using more medication, and seek a consultation with a mental health professional who is experienced in the psychological treatment—usually cognitive behavioral therapy—of anxiety disorders. If you're already in therapy, ask your therapist to coach you through the strategies in this book. With a bit more support, you might be able to stabilize your medication usage and continue with the recovery from your anxiety disorder.

FIND A COACH

The strategies in this book will help you recover from your anxiety disorder, but only if you practice them often. Because of your anxiety and avoidance, you might find it difficult to follow through with some of the strategies, particularly stepping toward discomfort. Often, it makes sense to find a coach to support you through the particularly rough points in your recovery.

How a Coach Can Help

A coach can help you in several ways. During your "stepping toward discomfort" practice, a coach can help you stay in an uncomfortable situation until you begin to feel less anxious. A coach can be particularly helpful when your goal is to step toward an object or situation that you fear and have avoided for many years. For example, if you wish to overcome a fear of heights, a coach can stand on a balcony with you until your fear decreases. If you're afraid to fly, a coach can accompany you on flights. In particular, you'll find that it helps to have someone coach you through the first few steps toward the feared object or situation, particularly at the beginning of your recovery, when you wonder whether you can do it.

A coach can help you gather the items you need for the "stepping toward discomfort" (*exposure*) practice. For example, if you're afraid of spiders or needles, a coach can gather these things for you because you're too afraid to gather them yourself. In addition, your coach can help you come up with steps on your "stepping toward discomfort" ladder. You'll learn more about this in chapter 6 ("Stepping toward Discomfort"), but it can help to have another person with whom you can brainstorm the small steps to include on your ladder.

A coach can demonstrate the step on your ladder before you try it. Observing your coach performing an activity or approaching an object or situation that frightens you can help decrease your fear. Experts call this *modeling*. Modeling helps because our fear of doing things diminishes when we repeatedly watch someone do the same things fearlessly. For example, if you're terrified of dirt or germs and a step on your ladder is to touch a countertop without washing your hands afterward, the coach can do this first, as you watch him respond fearlessly. Of course, this means that the coach must not fear the same things that you do.

Last, a coach can remind you to practice the many strategies in this book. Remember, though, the coach is there to support you as you recover from your anxiety disorder, not to do it for you. You, not your coach, are in charge of your recovery. A coach can also help you make time to practice, perhaps by watching your children for fifteen minutes or by running to the store for you, in order to allow you an hour to practice a step on your ladder.

Finding the Right Coach

A psychotherapist with experience in cognitive behavioral therapy for anxiety disorders is the best coach. If you're already working with a psychotherapist, she can assist you with the strategies in this book and help you stay on course. If you're not working with a psychotherapist, you can consult with one at any point in this book to help you practice what you're learning. If that isn't possible, perhaps ask a trusted friend, spouse, or relative to coach you through your recovery. However, not all coaches are equal. For example, family members who are "up close and personal" with your anxiety disorder might not be able to separate your goals from their own. They might become frustrated with your progress and insist that you do more than you're ready to try. For this reason, sometimes it helps to find a coach who is a little removed from the day-to-day aspects of your anxiety disorder.

The right coach is supportive and knowledgeable about you and your anxiety disorder. This person will answer your questions because he has become an expert on your anxiety disorder. Ask your coach to read this book to become familiar with the strategies in it and to read additional information on websites devoted to providing accurate and up-to-date information about anxiety disorders, such as www.adaa.org (Anxiety and Depression Association of America) and ocfounda tion.org (International OCD Foundation). In addition, the right coach praises you when you make progress and shows empathy when you're having a tough time. The right coach also helps you see the humor in things. Humor helps you step back from the situation you're in and see things in a different light. Humor helps keep you from taking things too seriously.

The right coach, of course, doesn't fear what you fear. This person won't become overly distressed or anxious when you're anxious. The right coach knows that it's normal for people to cry, shake, or even scream when they're anxious. If you cry or scream, the right coach encourages you to continue the exposure, rather than to stop it, so that you have time to learn that what you fear will happen doesn't happen and, just as important, that you can handle the intense fear and anxiety you're feeling.

Last, the right coach understands and agrees that you're in charge of each step of your recovery. This person accepts that you decide when you begin and what you do. At the same time, the right coach doesn't give up too easily. When you hesitate or want to stop, a good coach will encourage you to continue in a calm and firm manner. The right coach is there to support you and your recovery, which includes encouraging you to continue when you doubt that you can.

The approach in this book can help you recover from your excessive anxiety or anxiety disorder, because you'll learn specific skills that target the common factors that maintain anxiety and avoidance. Whether you have social anxiety or generalized anxiety, the skills in this book can help.

The first chapter presents the features of an anxious response and explains the difference between a normal and natural anxious response and the anxious responses at the heart of an anxiety disorder. You'll learn about the different anxiety disorders and the parts of your anxious response.

CHAPTER 1

Anxiety, Avoidance, and Anxiety Disorders

Anxiety and avoidance are at the heart of any anxiety disorder. People with anxiety disorders have struggled with excessive anxiety and persistent and life-altering avoidance for many years. This chapter presents basic information about anxiety and avoidance. When the danger is real, anxiety and its related emotion, fear, are your friends, so avoidance—part of your anxious response—is appropriate and reasonable. However, when you see danger where it's not, this same anxiety and avoidance no longer help you survive, but instead make each day a bit harder. When this happens, you have crossed the line between helpful and unhelpful anxiety and avoidance. This might mean you have an anxiety disorder.

This chapter also describes the difference between anxiety and an anxiety disorder, and it describes the features of typical anxiety disorders with which this book can help. It then presents the parts of your anxious response and describes the skills introduced later in the book that target these particular parts.

ANXIETY AND AVOIDANCE

Anxiety and avoidance are normal and useful. They protect us, motivate us, and teach us. What might your life be like if you never felt anxious? If you never felt anxious, what would help you work harder to prepare for an exam or presentation? If you never felt anxious, what would teach you to cope more effectively with a challenge or threat if it happened again? What might happen if you weren't able to avoid what you believed to be dangerous? If you couldn't avoid what was dangerous, how would you get through the day? How would you survive to see another day, for that matter?

Anxiety

Anxiety is *not* about the here and now. It's about the future. Anxiety alerts us that we *might be in danger* and prepares us for the worst. Anxiety signals us to focus our attention and energies on what might happen. When we feel anxious, our minds and bodies move into a state of vigilance, and we begin to prepare for the worst. A college student begins to feel anxious several weeks before final exams. She starts to think through the process of studying and decides which subjects she will study first and when. She begins to review her notes and calls her friends to set up times to study together. She thinks through which questions might be on the exams and whether they might be in essay or short-answer form. She schedules a meeting with her geography professor to go over a few points that she doesn't understand. The night before her first exam, she goes to bed early, and the next morning she's up early to eat a good breakfast and go over her notes one last time. Anxiety pushes us to plan and prepare. Anxiety is an inevitable part of life, so long as life includes threats and dangers. Anxiety is evidence of our will to live, to prosper, and to transcend the things that threaten us—anxiety is a life force.

Fear sounds the alarm that we *are in danger*—not perhaps in the same way as with anxiety—and our minds and bodies then react immediately, without thought. If you're jogging and something darts into your field of vision, you immediately duck or move away. If you and a friend are walking down the sidewalk and turn a corner to suddenly face a bicyclist coming straight at you, you quickly jump off the sidewalk and pull your friend out of the way too—without thinking or hesitating. In these situations, your fear motivates you to take immediate action. You don't need to think about whether you might be in danger and what that danger might be. In fact, if you were to think about it—for even a few seconds—you and your friend might be hurt. When we feel fear, we don't think about escaping; we just do it—and it happens so quickly that we don't necessarily make the connection that we are in danger at all.

Avoidance

Avoidance and *avoidance behaviors* are the things you do or don't do to reduce your anxiety. If you can, you might *completely avoid* situations that you fear. For example, if you have social anxiety disorder, you might avoid speaking in meetings, raising your hand in class, or giving presentations. If you fear heights, you might avoid entering tall buildings or riding escalators. If you worry that you'll have a panic attack while driving on the freeway, you might drive on surface streets only. When you can't avoid an object, activity, or situation, you might leave or *escape* it as soon as you can. If you worry that people think you're boring, you might leave a dinner party or hide in the restroom. If you worry that you might have a panic attack at any moment, you might dash out of a theater or meeting. When you can't completely avoid the situation or leave it when you like, you might try *partial avoidance*, or *safety behaviors*, to lessen your anxiety. If you have social anxiety, you might avoid looking people in the eyes when you speak to them. If you fear heights, you might hold the handrail tightly and look straight ahead when riding escalators. If you fear certain physical sensations, you might distract yourself from the sensations by watching television or keeping busy. In addition to avoiding the objects, activities, and situations that make you anxious, you might avoid images and thoughts that are part of your anxious response, by trying to suppress them or replace them with positive ones. Avoidance is perhaps the most debilitating feature of your anxiety disorder. You not only avoid the objects and situations that trigger your anxiety, but also learn to avoid the anxiety itself. Avoiding your anxious response and the many situations and activities in which it arises paints you into a corner. Avoidance boxes you in and limits your life. In fact, your anxiety isn't the problem; your desire to avoid feeling anxious at all costs is the problem. Avoiding your anxious response makes it difficult for you to live a full and meaningful life.

ANXIETY DISORDERS

Anxiety disorders are different from the everyday anxiety that we all feel, because the anxiety is more intense, lasts longer, and interferes significantly with your day-to-day functioning. Although about one in twenty people in the United States has one of the following anxiety disorders, you might be one of the 8 percent (Brown and Barlow 2009) of people with symptoms that don't fit neatly into one of these diagnostic categories. This book can help you too, or help you even if you don't have an anxiety disorder but want to learn to lessen your anxiety and stress in general.

Generalized Anxiety Disorder

Tyra describes herself as a "part-time nanny and full-time worrier." She worries about the same things that other people do—finances, relationships, health, world events—but she worries too much and for too long. She works only part-time, because she feels overwhelmed by her anxiety and worries. She doesn't sleep well, because the moment she lies down, she starts worrying about the things she needs to do the next day. She feels irritable all the time and argues with her boyfriend over little things. She has chronic headaches and diarrhea. She would like to find a different job, but every time she thinks about looking, she starts to worry that she will never find something, and so she puts off looking. Besides her job worries, Tyra worries about her health, her family, and world events, such as global warming or the ups and downs of the financial markets. Most troubling, Tyra can't stop worrying when she wants to, and she feels powerless to delay worrying, even for a few minutes, when she's trying to do other things.

Panic Disorder

Roman is a successful attorney who prides himself on working harder and longer than any other attorney in his firm. Over the last few months, the firm has lost several big accounts, and the senior partners have pressured him and the other attorneys to bill more and more hours. During this time,

Roman's first child was born, and he hasn't been sleeping well because of the new baby and pressure from his wife to spend more time helping her with the newborn.

One morning on the way to work, as he rode the escalator from the subway to street level, Roman had his first panic attack. He clutched the handrail tightly, because he felt intensely dizzy and short of breath. Terrified that he would faint and fall from the escalator, Roman ran the last few steps off it to safety. He managed to work through the day, but over the next few weeks, he began to have panic attacks in other situations, such as while walking up stairs, riding the subway, and driving certain stretches of highway.

Most of his panic attacks have seemed to come "out of the blue," and Roman has begun to worry that he might feel intensely dizzy at any time and in any situation. Roman continues to ride the subway, but only to street-level stations that don't require him to ride an escalator. He then takes a cab from the station to the office, which adds an extra thirty minutes to his day. He has begun to avoid other situations, such as stairs, balconies, or multistory parking garages. When he has to climb stairs or use balconies, he holds the handrail tightly and doesn't look down. Roman has tried several ways to "control" his panic, such as breathing and medications. However, he continues to avoid the situations that trigger the frightening physical sensations, and as a result, his world grows smaller each month.

Social Anxiety Disorder

Rosey, a school teacher, has always been anxious about speaking in front of people. She worries intensely and excessively about what others think of her, particularly when she's in front of a group but also when she's talking to people whom she respects or who are in positions of authority, such as the principal at her school. Rosey loves to teach, and for many years, she experienced little anxiety when teaching younger children. However, when budget cuts forced her to take a job teaching high school, she began to dread entering the classroom.

One day, while lecturing to her class, she began to blush intensely on her face and neck. She felt unable to continue speaking and left the classroom. Rosey worried that this would happen again, so she started calling in sick when she felt too anxious and wearing heavier makeup to hide her blushing. She avoided wearing certain colors that she feared would make her face look redder.

Rosey missed many days of school but managed to get through the school year. However, throughout the summer, she worried that she might not get through the next year. She has begun to think that she isn't cut out to be a teacher, even though she loves teaching and it's the only thing she has ever really wanted to do.

Obsessive-Compulsive Disorder

Bart, a graduate student in chemistry, repeatedly washes his hands any time he thinks he has touched something that might have germs on it. When he washes, he does it in a specific and elaborate way to make certain he doesn't miss a spot. He begins with the little finger on his left hand and moves up and down the inside of that finger to the next. The process typically takes forty-five minutes, and often, the longer he washes, the more anxious he feels. Many times Bart stops washing only because he can no longer bear the pain in his shoulders or the loud and angry protests from his roommate, who wants to use the bathroom. The thoughts of germs and images of getting sick frustrate Bart, because they don't make sense—he knows that—but he can't seem to ignore them or get them out of his mind.

Specific Phobia

Avi still remembers vividly the day, twenty-seven years ago, when his fear of cats started. He was in first grade and had stepped out of the classroom for recess, when he saw a cat clutching a dog by its head, scratching viciously at the dog's eyes and ears. The cat screeched as the dog yelped and ran around the school yard, trying to shake the cat from its head. Avi was paralyzed with fear, but unable to take his eyes off the terrible battle in front of him.

Since then, Avi has avoided cats and any situation in which he might encounter one. Avi quickly changes the TV channel when he sees a commercial or program in which cats appear. He walks away from conversations about cats, and he crosses the street when he sees a pet shop ahead.

Only recently, when Avi took a job as a kitchen appliance technician, did the phobia become a problem. Now, he dreads going to work, because he worries about encountering a cat in one of the homes he visits as part of his job. He calls ahead and asks homeowners whether they have cats and whether they will keep them away from him—and this helps sometimes. However, not all homeowners are willing to do this, and even when they do, the cat manages to get into the kitchen sometimes. The last time this happened, Avi freaked and ran from the house as the homeowner watched in disbelief. Avi is now so anxious about visiting homes that he is considering quitting his job.

Post-Traumatic Stress Disorder

If you have post-traumatic stress disorder, you've become anxious and fearful after a traumatic event that was outside the normal range of human experience. Such traumatic events would create intense fear, terror, and hopelessness in anyone, and they include natural disasters, such as earthquakes, tornadoes, and fires; car and plane crashes; and violent crimes against you or your immediate family, such as rape or other assault. Symptoms of post-traumatic stress disorder can appear immediately or shortly after the traumatic event or can be delayed, beginning more than six months afterward.

THE PARTS OF YOUR ANXIOUS RESPONSE

Now that you understand the nature of anxiety and avoidance and the different kinds of anxiety disorders, it's time to look more closely at your anxious experience itself. When you're anxious, you might feel as if the volume knob that controls your mind and body were up all the way. You might feel awash with anxiety, your mind may chatter, and your body may tremble. You know that your mind and body are sending you a signal, but you can't decode it. It's all happening too fast and too intensely. The first step in managing your anxiety is to decode the anxious signal—that is, break it down into its basic parts.

Breaking down your anxious response can also put it at arm's length—at least a bit—which can help you feel less overwhelmed by it. In addition, breaking down your anxious response into its basic parts will help you understand everything else that follows, because the skills you'll learn later target each of the basic parts: anxious mind, anxious body, and anxious actions.

Anxious Mind

This part of your anxious response includes certain thoughts and images. Often, these anxious thoughts are "what ifs": *What if the cat attacks me? What if I fail the test and flunk out of college? What if I say the wrong thing and she thinks I'm weird?* Typically, certain objects or situations trigger these anxious thoughts, such as the cat, the test, and the social interaction in the previous examples. Sometimes, a physical sensation can trigger the anxious thoughts. For example, a person with a headache might think, *What if I have a brain tumor?* A person who feels anxious and light-headed while driving might think, *What if I have a panic attack or pass out and lose control of the car?*

Anxious Body

This part of your anxious response consists of your physical sensations and feelings. Your body reacts in certain ways when you're anxious. For example, when you're afraid, you might feel short of breath and your heart might race. When you're anxious, your palms might sweat and you might feel nauseous and dizzy. When your body is anxious, you are better prepared to spring into action. In fact, an anxious body means that your body is redistributing resources to enhance your performance and protect you from danger. Your heart beats faster to pump more oxygen to your legs and arms, enhancing your ability to escape or defend yourself. Simultaneously, the fluttery feeling in your stomach means that blood is flowing away from your gut to make more blood available to your muscles and mind. Our bodies—even our anxious bodies—are a wonderful thing. We don't even have to think about these natural responses. Our bodies do this for us—immediately and with the sole purpose of protecting us.

Anxious Actions

Every emotion has a behavioral tendency; that is, every emotion drives us to act in certain ways. When we feel angry, we strike out. When we feel sad, we slow down and signal to others that we need support and comfort. When we feel anxious, we become more careful. At a party with people we don't know well, we might stick to safer topics or mingle less. When we feel anxious, we might also pace around the room or do other things to discharge some energy, such as bite our nails or organize our things. If our anxiety builds, we might even leave or escape the situation.

You've now learned the three basic parts of your anxious response: anxious mind, anxious body, and anxious actions. Many people are more aware of the signs of an anxious body than those of an anxious mind. Other people are aware of the signs of an anxious mind but unaware of the little (or big) things they do when they feel anxious. In fact, many very smart people are amazingly unaware of what they think and do when they're anxious, and this lack of awareness in certain situations often makes things much harder for them. For that reason, it's essential that you become an expert on the parts of your anxious response. These parts interact and feed off each other, so it's not always easy to break things down. However, everything you learn later in this book depends on your ability to understand and identify these parts—particularly when you're feeling anxious.

To help you with this, let's look at Rosey, the teacher with social anxiety disorder, and break down her anxious response when she approached the librarian to ask for help with finding a particular book (see sample exercise 1.1).

Sample Exercise 1.1 Rosey's Anxious-Response Worksheet

Anxious Response		
Anxious Mind **(Thoughts)**	**Anxious Body** **(Physical Sensations)**	**Anxious Actions** **(Behaviors)**
What if she sees that I'm blushing?	*My face and neck felt warm. I felt dizzy and nauseous, and my heart beat very fast.*	*I put on heavy makeup, just in case I would blush. I didn't look at her, and I quickly asked about the book and walked away. I pulled my collar up to hide my neck so that she couldn't see me blushing. When she asked if she could show me where the book was, I said no and looked for it myself, because I wanted to get away from her.*

Now, why don't you use the blank Anxious-Response Worksheet (see exercise 1.1) to break down your anxious response to a particular situation? If you can, select a situation that's still fresh in your mind. Then, over the next week or so, use this form to record one or two more situations in which you felt anxious. Any anxious response will do. You don't have to use situations in which you felt *very* anxious. In fact, you can often learn as much from situations in which your anxiety is low as you can from situations where your anxiety is high. Furthermore, low-anxiety situations tend to occur more often than do high-anxiety ones, so you're likely to catch more situations and get more practice breaking down your anxious responses when you practice with low-anxiety situations.

Exercise 1.1 Anxious-Response Worksheet

Anxious Response		
Anxious Mind (Thoughts)	**Anxious Body (Physical Sensations)**	**Anxious Actions (Behaviors)**

PRIMARY AND SECONDARY ANXIOUS RESPONSES, AND THE ANXIETY BOX

You've learned two things about your anxious response so far. Your anxious response is an ongoing interaction of your anxious mind (thoughts), anxious body (physical sensations), and anxious actions (behaviors); and your anxious response is a normal and natural emotional experience. At this point, you might ask, *If my anxious response is normal and natural, why am I suffering so much?* It might help to learn that there are two anxious responses at work: primary and secondary anxious responses.

Primary Anxious Response

Your *primary anxious response* (PAR) is your first response to a new and perhaps dangerous object, activity, or situation. Your PAR is an instinctive response to a real and present danger, or to what appears, at that moment, to be a real and present danger around you or even inside you, such as a physical sensation or an unpleasant or scary image. This is your fight-or-flight response, and without thinking, you instinctively escape (if you can), freeze (if you can't escape), or shield yourself somehow in order to protect yourself. Your PAR motivates you to act quickly, without thinking, and once you are out of danger or realize that you weren't really in danger, your PAR begins to dampen. Your body and mind calm. Your attention opens again, and your fear begins to fade.

Imagine that one day you step on the elevator in your office building. The doors close and the elevator moves slowly downward, the way it has countless times over the years. Today, though, the elevator jerks, drops two feet, and stops. This triggers your primary anxious response, so your body tenses, your heart rate increases, and your attention shifts and narrows on the elevator. *Is it still dropping?* You listen and wait. You quickly think through what you might do if it happens again. Your PAR is in charge. The elevator begins to move again, and in a minute, the doors open and you step off. You're safe, and with that realization, your PAR begins to fade. Your body slows down. Your mind clears, enabling you to think about other things. You enter the office and tell a few colleagues about your experience. You notify the building manager, who responds that he will call a technician to inspect the elevator. In fifteen minutes, you're working, laughing with colleagues, and on to other things. Your PAR worked perfectly, just as it has before. At lunch, you speak to the building manager again, who tells you that there was a minor problem with the cable. You learn that you were never really in danger and that the technician adjusted the cable so that it's not likely to happen again.

Secondary Anxious Response

At the end of the day, you head out of the office for the elevator but hesitate at the door. Your *secondary anxious response* (SAR) is now in charge. You remember what the building manager told you: the elevator is fine, you were never in real danger, and it's not likely to happen again. Still, you're a bit worried. You consider taking the stairs, but then the elevator doors open, you watch colleagues step on, and the doors close. You step back and watch another group of colleagues take the elevator. Everything appears to be fine: no danger, no threat. You press the "down" button, and the elevator doors open. Your body is tense, and your palms are sweating a little. Your heart beats quickly as you slowly step inside the elevator. You stand near the back rather than near the door, because you think that might be safer. The doors close and you feel anxious. You listen carefully for any unusual sound. The elevator continues to move down. It doesn't drop. All appears to be fine. The elevator doors open, you step off, and your mind and body quickly calm. However, for the next few days, each time you step onto the elevator, you feel a little anxious. Day by day, however, your anxiety lessens. Sometimes your mind remembers the day the elevator dropped suddenly, but you remind yourself that you were never really in danger, that it dropped only a couple of feet and that everything is fine. After a while, you find yourself daydreaming on the elevator the way you used to, without wondering whether the elevator might drop again and without experiencing a rapid heartbeat. This is your secondary anxious response in action, but because it's flexible, it adapts to the reality of the situation. Your thoughts, your attention, and your actions return to what is normal and appropriate. This is your SAR at its best.

Your secondary anxious response is composed of the same components (anxious mind, anxious body, and anxious action) as your PAR, but it arises *after* the experience. Your SAR prepares you for the same threat or danger that triggered your PAR. For most people, secondary anxious responses usually are as adaptive as primary anxious responses. A SAR only becomes a problem when it's stuck in a pattern that you can't change. People who have anxiety disorders have secondary anxious responses that have become inflexible, at least about certain objects, activities, or situations. They can't shift or change their secondary anxious responses to the reality of the situation. An inflexible SAR causes you to think, feel, and act in the same way, regardless of the reality of the situation. The inflexibility of your SAR makes it difficult for you to relax, to learn that you're not in danger, and to live a full and meaningful life.

The Anxiety Box

People with anxiety disorders have inflexible secondary anxious responses that box them into a particular way of thinking, feeling, and acting. This is the *anxiety box*, and the goal of this book is to help you learn to shift out of this pattern when you wish so that you can see things as they really are. Now look at Roman's anxiety box (see figure 1.1).

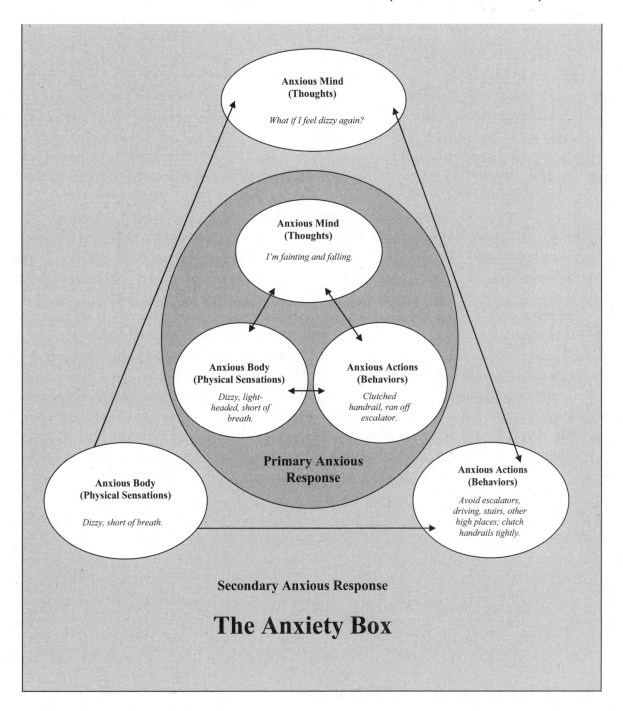

Figure 1.1 Roman's Primary and Secondary Anxious Responses, and the Anxiety Box

Roman's primary anxious response occurred one day while riding the escalator. He had been anxious and stressed for many months, and on this day, he felt light-headed. Perhaps he was light-headed because he hadn't slept much in the past few days. The demands of his job and new baby certainly caused him to feel anxious and stressed. Regardless of the reason for the dizzy feeling, he thought that he might pass out and fall down the escalator, so he panicked. He feared not only that he might hurt himself but also the humiliation that falling in a public place would cause him.

Afterward, Roman's secondary anxious response kicked in. He kept worrying about feeling dizzy and passing out while riding the escalator, and he also began to worry that he might pass out in other situations, such as when climbing the stairs or driving. If Roman's SAR were flexible, he'd learn, after a few days of doing what he typically does throughout the day, that he didn't pass out when he felt dizzy. Furthermore, if Roman's SAR were flexible, he'd understand that if he did pass out in public, it wouldn't be the end of the world. He'd understand that he could handle the embarrassment he'd feel and that the embarrassment, regardless of how intense, would pass too.

Roman has panic disorder because his secondary anxious response is stuck. He lives in the anxiety box of a rigid pattern of thinking, attending, and acting in the same ways day after day. Although the SAR is as normal and natural a response as the primary anxious response, it can become a problem when it's stuck.

The purpose of both our primary and secondary anxious responses is to protect us from the threats and challenges of life. For some people, however, the natural and normal SAR creates problems. These people are stuck in their secondary anxious responses—trapped in the anxiety box— and because they're unable to move out of it, they have an anxiety disorder.

The next chapter provides more information about the parts of your secondary anxious response, setting the stage for you to become an expert on the nature of your particular anxiety box. Using the skills in this book, you'll gain greater influence over your SAR, and with this new flexibility, you'll break free from the anxiety box that has limited your life and caused you years of suffering.

CHAPTER 2

Watching and Learning

Now that you understand the three parts of an anxious response—anxious mind, anxious body, and anxious actions—and have used them to identify what you're thinking, feeling, and doing when you're anxious, we will look at the full picture of your anxious responses, particularly your secondary anxious responses. In this chapter and the remainder of the book, "anxious response" or even "anxiety box" refers to your secondary anxious response.

This chapter will teach you how to watch your secondary anxious responses in order to learn what triggers them (the antecedents) and what happens afterward (the consequences). The antecedents and consequences that bracket any anxious response make up the "ARC" (Barlow et al. 2011) of anxiety. It's particularly important that you understand the consequences of your anxious responses, because they're likely your reasons for deciding to work toward mastering your anxiety and avoidance. The chapter then describes typical consequences of avoidance and other anxious actions and helps you identify some of the consequences you might experience.

WHY WATCH AND LEARN?

There are a number of good reasons to watch and learn from your anxious responses. First, as you watch and learn, you practice stepping out of your secondary anxious response—if only for a moment—to observe rather than react. In a sense, you practice climbing above your anxious response to look down on the overwhelming feelings of anxiety and panic that might be swirling around you. From this new perspective, you learn when, where, and why you had the SAR, which can lessen the intensity of your anxiety and make other secondary anxious responses more manageable.

Second, through watching and learning, you'll understand that your anxiety doesn't come out of nowhere—even if it feels that way sometimes—and instead, you'll learn that your secondary anxious responses are quite predictable. You'll discover that this new understanding reassures you and lessens the intensity of your anxious responses.

Third, you might have learned things over the years that cause you to act in certain ways—things that you're not even fully aware that you've learned—and through watching and learning you'll realize that certain ways you act create problems for you. Understanding the consequences of your secondary anxious responses to you and others will motivate you to persist through difficult moments of mastering your anxious responses.

Last, you can learn the best skills in the world to manage your anxiety, but they won't do you any good if you don't know when to use them. Through watching and learning, you'll become an expert on your secondary anxious responses. In particular, you might learn that you're anxious more often than you thought. You might discover that there are little anxious moments that aren't even on your radar. Catching these moments is essential, because some of the skills you'll learn later in the book will work best when you catch your SAR, when the anxiety is low and you can more effectively apply what you've learned.

THE ARC OF ANXIETY

Although they might not seem so, your secondary anxious responses are predictable. Some event or situation triggers every anxious episode you have. These triggers are the *antecedents* (A) of your anxious responses. Once an event or situation triggers your anxious *response* (R), you experience some *consequence* (C) from it. Every anxious episode, then, has an *ARC* (Barlow et al. 2011). The ARC is a very effective way to learn more about your anxiety and fear:

*A*ntecedent or trigger: An antecedent is the event that precedes your anxious response. For example, if you're afraid to speak in public, an antecedent (A) might be your boss informing you that you must present to your work team.

*R*esponse to the antecedent: This is your anxious response, and it includes the three parts you have learned: anxious mind, anxious body, and anxious actions.

*C*onsequence: This is the consequence or consequences of your anxious response. For example, if you avoided attending the team meeting (your anxious action) and your boss later reprimanded you for missing it, this is a consequence of your anxious response. At times, the consequences might be short term, such as experiencing several hours or days of distress after an event or cutting short a performance or activity. At other times, the consequences might be long term, such as losing a job because you're chronically late or often call in sick. Other long-term consequences might include increased stress from overpreparing for a task or chronic insomnia from worrying.

Now, let's look at several anxious episodes and use ARC to understand each of them. Let's begin with Rosey, the teacher with social anxiety disorder who worried about speaking to her class and others, particularly after she began to blush. Rosey is in charge of organizing the community-service awards given annually to three students and three teachers. Her principal asked Rosey to say a few words to the audience and hand out the awards.

Rosey stands onstage in the auditorium. The stage is about four feet high, and she's at the podium looking out over the assembled students and teachers. She's nervous and begins to worry that she has started to blush. Her face and neck feel warm, and she can't get out of her mind that she's as red as a beet and that everyone is looking at her. She feels nauseous and her heart races. As she looks out over the audience, she's sure that the students and other teachers can see that she's blushing. She thinks that they know she's terrified and that they think she's weird. She manages to get through the presentation, but cuts it short. She leaves early and calls in sick the next day.

All day long and for the next few days, she's upset with herself. Rosey is certain that she made a fool of herself, and she tells her principal that she no longer wants to organize school events. In addition, she informs the principal that she's considering making this her final year of teaching. Rosey's ARC Worksheet looks like this (see sample exercise 2.1a):

Sample Exercise 2.1a Rosey's ARC Worksheet

Antecedents	Anxious Response		Consequences
	Anxious Mind (Thoughts)	Anxious Body (Physical Sensations) / Anxious Actions (Behaviors)	
What happened just before your anxious response? Where were you? What was going on? What were you doing or thinking? What internal sensations got your attention?			What happened after your anxious response? Did you experience some internal consequence (guilt, anger, shame, sleeplessness)? Did you experience some external consequence (criticism, anger toward you, lecture)?
Announcing winners of the community service awards. I'm standing onstage at the podium.	What if they see that I'm blushing?	My face and neck feel warm; dizzy, nauseous; my heart races. / I cut the presentation short. I told the principal that I don't want to organize events again and that this year may be my last year of teaching.	I'm upset and angry with myself for cutting the presentation short. / I worry all day about what I'll do if I give up teaching.

Roman, the attorney with panic disorder, fears feeling dizzy or light-headed. He is giving a brief presentation to a meeting of a local organization of lawyers. He's standing at the podium on the stage, which is about four feet high. Roman didn't sleep well last night, from worry about having another panic attack during his presentation. As Roman looks down to the audience below, he begins to feel intensely dizzy. He grips the sides of the podium, convinced that he might faint at any moment. His heart beats furiously, and he's sweating and short of breath. Roman cuts the presentation short and abruptly leaves the stage and auditorium. He calls his wife to pick him up. All that night he worries what his colleagues and senior partners might say about his leaving the meeting. He's certain that his days at the firm are numbered, so he calls in sick for the next three days. He refuses to return calls from a senior partner who wonders how he's feeling. Roman's ARC looks like this (see sample exercise 2.1b):

Sample Exercise 2.1b Roman's ARC Worksheet

Antecedents	Anxious Response		Consequences
	Anxious Mind (Thoughts)	Anxious Body (Physical Sensations)	Anxious Actions (Behaviors)
What happened just before your anxious response? Where were you? What was going on? What were you doing or thinking? What internal sensations got your attention?				What happened after your anxious response? Did you experience some internal consequence (guilt, anger, shame, sleeplessness)? Did you experience some external consequence (criticism, anger toward you, lecture)?
I look down from the stage as I'm giving a presentation, and feel dizzy.	What if I faint?	Dizzy, my heart beats fast, and I feel faint; sweating; short of breath.	I cut the presentation short. I called my wife to pick me up. I called in sick three days. I didn't return the senior partner's calls.	I'm upset and ashamed about leaving. I worry all night that I've ruined my career. My colleagues are frustrated with me, because they have to do my work.

The ARCs of Rosey and Roman are interesting in that they share the same antecedent (A), giving a presentation, yet their anxious responses are unique. This often happens. Your anxious response to a particular situation or antecedent might be very different from that of someone else. This is because our anxious responses depend on what is important or most distressing about particular elements of the antecedent. In Rosey's case, the important element of the antecedent was that students and teachers were scrutinizing or watching her. Unlike Rosey, Roman was anxious not about speaking in public but about looking down from the stage, which triggered the dizzy feelings that he feared would cause him to pass out or would provoke another panic attack.

Furthermore, an antecedent (A) can be an event or situation that just happened, happened earlier in the day, or happened even last week or last month. For example, an antecedent can be a consequence from a previous anxious episode. If, all night long, you worried about the consequences from the day before and awakened tired and out of sorts, your fatigue might be the antecedent for your next anxious episode. You might begin to worry about how you'll perform at work because you're tired. Similarly, an antecedent can be a memory from the night or day before, or sometimes several weeks before. For example, you might remember how you left a meeting because you felt too anxious, and now the antecedent includes not only today's meeting, but also the memory of how you left last week's meeting. Now, use the following form to watch and learn about your own ARCs (see exercise 2.1).

Exercise 2.1 ARC Worksheet

Antecedents	Anxious Response		Consequences
	Anxious Mind (Thoughts)	Anxious Body (Physical Sensations)	Anxious Actions (Behaviors)
What happened just before your anxious response? Where were you? What was going on? What were you doing or thinking? What internal sensations got your attention?				What happened after your anxious response? Did you experience some internal consequence (guilt, anger, shame, sleeplessness)? Did you experience some external consequence (criticism, anger toward you, lecture)?

TYPES OF ANXIOUS ACTIONS

Anxious actions generally take two forms: avoiding the objects and situations that trigger your anxious response, and neutralizing your anxiety through some activity or action. People might use several of these anxious actions simultaneously, regardless of the anxiety disorder that troubles them. Whatever anxious actions you use, the goal of any anxious action is to give you some short-term relief. However, the problems that accompany relying on anxious actions to manage your anxiety are not short term. They're long term and life altering.

Avoidance

People with anxiety disorders avoid, when they can, the things that trigger their anxious responses. If you anticipate encountering something that's likely to trigger your anxious response, you'll make a plan to avoid it. If you can't avoid it, however, you'll think of how to escape from it as soon as you can.

SITUATIONAL AND OBJECT AVOIDANCE

This is the most common type of avoidance. If you're afraid of dogs, you avoid not only dogs (object), but also places where you're likely to see them, such as the local dog park or pet supply stores (situations). With situational and object avoidance, you stay away from the people, places, things, or even activities that tend to trigger your anxious response. People avoid situations and objects in little ways, such as avoiding eye contact with people, or in big ways, such as staying away from crowds or parties. If particular places or activities trigger your anxious response, such as panicky feelings, you might avoid particular environments or certain places within them. For example, if theaters trigger your anxious response, you might avoid theaters altogether or avoid sitting in the middle of a row or a front row. If you're afraid that something might be wrong with your heart or lungs, you might avoid climbing stairs, jogging, or even walking briskly.

SOMATIC AVOIDANCE

With somatic avoidance, you avoid triggering the sensations associated with your anxious body, such as a racing heart, breathlessness, feeling flushed, sweating, or trembling. For example, if you felt short of breath when you had a panic attack, you might move more slowly or exercise less regularly, because when you exercise, you feel short of breath, a sensation that frightens you. You might even avoid pleasant sensations, such as sexual arousal or excitement about a party or upcoming event, because you can't be certain that these sensations are not ones you fear.

COGNITIVE AVOIDANCE

This kind of avoidance, as the saying goes, is all in your head. You might avoid thinking certain things that make you feel anxious. You might avoid distressing memories, such as feeling embarrassed at a party several years ago. You might avoid images that make you anxious, such as your boss yelling at you or images of you doing something you would never do. You might push the unwanted thought, memory, or image out of your mind or try to distract yourself by thinking or doing something else. You might avoid thinking about something really scary—such as losing your job—by worrying about less scary things, like whether you'll finish a work project on time or whether your boss likes you.

Neutralization

This form of anxious action includes the small and big things you do to try to eliminate any danger and risk. You might check locks, light switches, and the stove, even when you know you turned them off—just in case. You might wash your hands repeatedly to try to eliminate any chance of getting ill. You might overprepare for a test, or you might work and rework an assignment in order to avoid mistakes at any cost. Furthermore, you might try to neutralize your anxious response by replacing it with another emotion that, in some way, is less distressing than feeling anxious. For example, you might replace your anxiety with frustration or the excitement of video games, gambling, or Internet porn. Similarly, you might try to neutralize your anxious response by pushing it aside with food, alcohol, or drugs. You might try to neutralize a distressing thought or image by replacing it with some other mental content, such as a good image to counter a bad one. Similarly, you might fill your mind with fantasies or daydreams to distract yourself, or you might repeat certain words or phrases to neutralize a frightening thought or image or simply to feel slightly less anxious in general. Some people use prayer or positive affirmations in this way, hoping that it will prevent the bad thing from happening or simply give them a moment of relief from their anxiety.

TYPICAL CONSEQUENCES OF ANXIOUS ACTIONS

Although your anxious actions provide you with some short-term relief from your anxiety and fear, they set you up for long-term pain. Perhaps the biggest consequence of anxious actions is that they prevent you from learning something that would help you feel less anxious in the future. Suppose you're in a class, preparing for an exam. Your teacher is well meaning but ill informed about a particular topic and teaches you some incorrect information that you then apply during the exam. You fail the exam, not because you didn't study enough or aren't smart enough, but because you learned something that you thought was correct but wasn't. We all learn things that we have no reason to question, so for that reason, we continue to act as if they were correct.

This is true about anxiety too. Our anxious responses are there to teach us, and we might not stop to question whether or not what they teach us about the world and ourselves is correct. Why would we? However, when you repeatedly act on incorrect information from your previous anxious response, you fail to learn that the world is safer than you think and that you're more capable than you believe. If you believe that all dogs bite and you then avoid all dogs, you never learn that not all dogs bite. Furthermore, because you avoid all dogs, you might never learn an appropriate response to meeting a strange dog, such as asking the owner whether the dog is safe to pet before reaching out to pet it. If you believe that you can't handle your anxious feelings and that they will overwhelm you, and you then leave the situation, you never learn that you can handle your panicky feelings and that they not only don't overwhelm you, but also will pass in time. Furthermore, if you begin to avoid any situation that makes you even a little anxious, then you don't learn important information about how anxiety really works: that it goes up and down, but always comes down, and that whether it's up or down, you can always handle it.

Consequences differ for each person and each episode. A consequence might be short term and perhaps not particularly bad in and of itself. However, other consequences might be long term. They not only affect your life day to day, but also build until each day of your life becomes harder and the scope of your life narrower. If you have a long-term pattern of anxious actions, you likely have a life filled with long-term consequences. There are three types of long-term consequences of anxious actions.

Emotional Consequences

People caught in a pattern of anxious actions often feel sad, guilty, frustrated, or ashamed. If you're late for work because you must repeatedly check all the doors and windows in your home, you might feel frustrated with yourself and think you're a loser. You might feel deeply embarrassed that you can't do things that your friends do, because you're too anxious or fearful. You might feel deeply ashamed of some of your thoughts and behaviors, but powerless to stop them. You might feel guilty about disappointing your friends and family again, because you were too anxious to attend an important function. These emotional consequences start small, but year after year, their weight builds until you don't like yourself much and may spend more and more time alone.

Relationship and Family Consequences

Anxious actions can damage once loving and caring relationships. Your friends and family might have been patient with your anxious responses at first. They might have said, "Oh, well, that's just how Marcie is," but over time, they have become less patient and less forgiving when you cancel attending an event at the last minute. You might hear from your friends less often, either because they know you'll say no or because they're angry or upset with your continued reluctance to try things that make you anxious. Your partner might feel burdened by your dependency on her to drive you everywhere or to make excuses to your boss when you're too anxious to go to work. Your children might feel disappointed that you don't attend their ball games or school performances because open spaces or auditoriums make you anxious. Those who care about you might have resigned themselves to having half a father, half a husband, or half a friend, and even if they don't reveal their anger or disappointment, you can feel it, which makes you even more anxious and upset with yourself.

Work or Professional Consequences

Anxious actions can cause long-term consequences in your work. If you're too anxious to be assertive, you might find that you don't advance as quickly as your colleagues do, even though you're as capable and hardworking as they are. Your boss might threaten to fire you for chronic lateness, not knowing that you're late due to your fear of driving and the need to take multiple buses to get to work. You might risk demotion because you're too anxious to speak in public, or you might have taken a job for which you're overqualified and that bores you, just to avoid giving presentations at work.

Health Consequences

Anxious actions can cause long-term health consequences too. You might skip meals or eat fast food out of worry over potentially missing a deadline or failing to complete the day's work. Now, you've gained so much weight that your back and legs hurt, and you're on blood-pressure medications. You might have started to drink a glass or two of wine at night to help you unwind and get to sleep, but now you're worried that the wine worsens your anxiety and sleep; nevertheless, you can't seem to cut back. When you're anxious, you might bite your nails until they bleed or pull your hair to the point of embarrassment, but you can't seem to stop.

Through your anxious actions, you fail to learn that you've less to fear than you think, which is why your life grows smaller and more difficult. The biggest long-term consequence of anxious actions, however, is that you end up not living, because you're too afraid to live fully and actively.

SELF-ASSESSMENT: CONSEQUENCES OF YOUR ANXIOUS ACTIONS

Now, review the ARC Worksheet you completed earlier, or go ahead and complete several new ones. Referring again to the ARC acronym, pay attention to your anxious *actions* (as part of your anxious *response*) and the short-term and long-term *consequences* of your anxious responses. It's the relentless accumulation of these consequences—whether they're short term or long term, small or large—that affects people in big ways. Consequence after consequence, over many years, erodes your self-esteem, undercuts your self-confidence, and leads to relationship and work problems. Rosey took a few minutes to examine both the short-term and long-term consequences of her anxious actions. This exercise was quite helpful for Rosey. She learned that some consequences were quite clear, but others, such as the worry and shame she feels when she avoids, were new to her (see sample exercise 2.2).

Sample Exercise 2.2 Rosey's Self-Assessment: Consequences of Anxious Actions

Anxious Action	Emotional Consequences	Relationship and Family Consequences	Work or Professional Consequences	Health Consequences	Other Consequences
Situational: Avoid certain people, places, activities, or things	I feel ashamed when I can't do something because I'm anxious. I feel guilty because I depend too much on my husband.	If I give up teaching, we can't afford things that are fun or good for our family. My husband has to make excuses for me, which upsets him.	I can't give presentations or make announcements. I can't share my ideas with more than a few people at a time.		
Somatic: Avoid internal sensations, such as blushing, breathlessness, increased heart rate, sexual arousal	I feel ashamed and worried when I think I'm blushing.	I won't do things with my husband if I think I might blush.	I can't give presentations or make announcements because I'm afraid I'll blush. I won't do social things with the teachers because I'm worried they think I'm weird.	I've started to exercise less because I'm afraid I'll blush more.	I can't wear pretty, bright colors because it will make my face look red.

Anxious Action	Emotional Consequences	Relationship and Family Consequences	Work or Professional Consequences	Health Consequences	Other Consequences
Cognitive: Avoid certain thoughts, images, or memories	*I get really upset with myself any time I think about blushing.* *I feel very ashamed when I think about the times I've blushed.*				*Any time someone even mentions blushing or feeling embarrassed, I walk away, which is rude and awkward.*
Neutralization: Things you do to neutralize anxiety or distress, such as seek reassurance, use drugs or alcohol, engage in checking, reason with yourself repeatedly, seek a stronger emotion to cover the anxiety or fear	*I check mirrors or my reflection in mirrors in certain situations to make certain I'm not blushing, which annoys me.*	*I constantly ask my husband if I'm blushing, which frustrates him.* *I ask my husband or mother to speak to people for me or do things for me, which frustrates them and makes their lives harder.*	*I ask the other teachers questions to see what they really think of me, but this makes me look like I am not very confident and don't know what I'm doing.*	*I overeat, especially at night.*	
Other:					
Other:					

Now, use the following worksheet to assess the short-term and long-term consequences of your own anxious actions. Like Rosey, pay attention to all the consequences of your anxious actions, both short and long term. Although some consequences are short term, many short-term consequences can lead to long-term ones, such as losing your job or choosing work that causes you less anxiety but is boring and unfulfilling (see exercise 2.2).

Exercise 2.2 Self-Assessment: Consequences of Anxious Actions

Anxious Action	Emotional Consequences	Relationship and Family Consequences	Work or Professional Consequences	Health Consequences	Other Consequences
Situational: Avoid certain people, places, activities, or things					
Somatic: Avoid internal sensations, such as blushing, breathlessness, increased heart rate, sexual arousal					
Cognitive: Avoid certain thoughts, images, or memories					

Neutralization: Things you do to neutralize anxiety or distress, such as seek reassurance, use drugs or alcohol, engage in checking, reason with yourself repeatedly, seek a stronger emotion to cover the anxiety or fear				
Other:				
Other:				

Watching and learning about your anxious responses is a powerful first step in mastering your anxiety and avoidance. In addition to understanding the "what, when, and why" of your anxious responses, you've learned about the short-term and long-term consequences of your anxious actions. These consequences have created a life that's harder and more limited than necessary, and they might be the reason why you're reading this book. However, an awareness of the consequences of your anxious actions might not be enough to keep you going as you tackle the hard work of mastering your anxiety.

The next chapter presents the essential role that motivation plays in recovery from excessive anxiety or an anxiety disorder. You'll learn the typical roadblocks to motivation and two strategies that can keep you moving forward with your recovery plan: analyzing the pluses and minuses of changing versus remaining the same, and clarifying your values.

CHAPTER 3

Moving Forward

Moving forward means committing to breaking free from the cycle of anxiety and avoidance that has robbed you of a full and meaningful life. If you're like many people with an anxiety disorder, you've been stuck in this cycle for years. So moving forward will take considerable motivation and hard work on your part. This chapter presents the role of motivation in your recovery from anxiety and avoidance. You'll start by learning some facts about motivation that will help keep your recovery on course. The chapter then describes two motivation-enhancement strategies—analyzing your decisions (examining the pluses and minuses of changing versus staying the same) and clarifying your core values. You'll also find a number of exercises to help you maintain your motivation through the inevitable ups and downs of your recovery.

MOTIVATION

Motivation is an essential ingredient in any recovery plan. The more motivated you are to overcome your anxiety and avoidance, the more likely you are to practice the skills in this book until they become second nature to you. Furthermore, the more motivated you are to change, the more likely you are to develop a new attitude toward your anxiety and avoidance that will help you get better and stay better.

But as important as motivation is to any recovery, people often misunderstand it. Before we move to the ways in which you can increase your motivation, let's look at motivation—what it is and is not.

Adequate motivation is enough. If you're one of those people who believes you can't start recovering until you're very motivated, then you're stuck. Motivation doesn't operate like a toggle switch that you turn on or off: switch on and you do it, switch off and you don't. Instead, motivation operates more like a dimmer switch: you can turn it off, but you can also change the level of "on"—from a little on to intensely on. In fact, you require only as much motivation as is necessary for you to try, whether "trying" means trying or practicing a new skill, or stopping behavior that you've learned is unhelpful. Adequate motivation is about willingness in the moment. In other words, you need only enough motivation to do something in that moment, and those moments add up. So, when you consider how much motivation you need to recover from your anxiety disorder, don't think about weeks or months of working hard—although it might take that long. Instead, consider how much motivation you need to practice a new skill today or even in this moment.

Motivation changes. Motivation isn't constant, but fluctuates over time. At times, your motivation will be high, and you'll move ahead in your recovery—perhaps two or three steps—and feel thrilled at how easy it all was. Then the next day, your motivation will drop, and what was effortless the day before is harder now. At those times, it takes greater willingness on your part to move ahead even a half step. Many factors nudge your motivation up or down. You might feel sick or more tired than usual. Your stress at work might have increased. Maybe you argued with a friend or your partner the night before. You might be in a good place, with little anxiety, and think, *Things are okay now, so why push it?*

In other words, even when your motivation is adequate to begin your recovery, this doesn't mean it will stay that way. Your motivation might increase or decrease in a day, an hour, or even a minute. This is a normal and natural part of the recovery process. Don't give up when your motivation decreases. Instead, look for ways to break things down, or try again what you practiced and mastered last week or last month. Find something that you're willing to try, and start there. In other words, don't stop trying; try something else.

Realistic expectations enhance motivation. Realistic personal expectations decrease anxiety and enhance motivation, partly because if your expectations are realistic, you're more likely to achieve them. For example, imagine that you're a high jumper standing at the line waiting to jump. The stadium is full of fans, who are all watching you. The pole is set at 7 feet 2 inches. Your personal best is 6 feet 6 inches (the world record is about 8 feet). You look at the pole and think, *That's 8 inches higher than my personal best. There's not much chance I'll jump an additional 8 inches. Maybe I could make 1 or 2 inches over my personal best, but 8 inches? I don't think so.* Your anxiety increases. You hesitate but know you must try, because all eyes are on you. You run toward the pole, but your heart isn't in it. You've already given up. Now instead imagine that the pole had been set at 6 feet 7 inches, one inch higher than your personal best. You look at the pole this time and think, *That's just 1 inch higher than my personal best, just 1 inch. It's a stretch, but I think I can do it. I was close last time—so close; perhaps this is the day.* Your anxiety is reasonable. You don't hesitate. In fact, you look forward to the challenge. You run toward the pole with the attitude that this is your day; you can do it.

Throughout your recovery, it's essential that you set realistic expectations about the process and your participation in it. One day you'll practice a skill and find it easy. The next day it's harder. This is normal and natural. Change is an up-and-down process, and it's unrealistic to expect to always be on top of things or to always be as successful as you were the day before.

Motivation increases as you succeed. Nothing succeeds like success, and nothing erodes willingness and motivation more than failing, partly because nothing builds confidence more than success. The more confident we are, the less anxious we feel and the more willing we are to try again. This book introduces one skill after another, each building on the one before. As you master one skill, the next one might seem less daunting, so you might be more motivated to try again. This approach is particularly important when you learn to face your fears later in the book (chapter 6, "Stepping toward Discomfort"). You'll face your fears in small, manageable steps that will help you succeed, and as you succeed, your confidence and motivation will increase too.

True motivation is an invitation, not a push. True motivation is not a push. Motivation is not doing something because you think you should or others think you should. True motivation is a willingness to try because you recognize and accept that it makes sense for you to change. People who do something because they think they should feel pressured and more anxious. After all, who likes for someone to push them toward something that scares them? Imagine that you're standing on a footbridge that swings a thousand feet above the valley floor. The bridge is missing two slats, and you must leap a two-foot gap to move ahead. You hesitate as you look down. You're afraid. The hiker in front has already crossed, and leans forward, his hand outstretched, inviting you to try. "It'll be fine," he tells you. Your fear lessens, and your willingness increases. *Yes, it'll be fine*, you tell yourself, and you leap. The day before, another traveler on that same footbridge faced the same two-foot gap, but the hiker behind him pushed him toward the gap. "Hurry, we don't have all day. Just jump," he said. This traveler felt the push and the pressure. His fear increased and he began to back away. The hiker pushed the traveler toward the gap harder and more forcefully. The traveler panicked and backed away. He wasn't jumping that day and no one could make him. Motivation is an invitation, not a push.

PLUSES AND MINUSES OF CHANGE

During your recovery, when your motivation decreases, you can get back on track by reminding yourself of the reasons why you decided to move forward with recovery in the first place. Examining the pluses and minuses of changing versus staying the same is *decisional analysis*. When you avoid, you likely overfocus on the reasons to stay the same. Over and over, you convince yourself that staying the same isn't so bad: *Driving an extra hour to work to avoid the freeway isn't so bad. It's just an hour. I can spare an hour. It's not that important that I attend Gloria's birthday party. She'll understand.* Decisional analysis opens the lens somewhat so that you can fully examine all the pluses and minuses of starting your recovery. Change begins when you have thoughtfully weighed the reasons to change against reasons to stay the same. In this way, you take control of your recovery, because you make the choice yourself.

Let's look at Roman's Pluses and Minuses Worksheet (sample exercise 3.1). Roman spent a few minutes writing the pluses and minuses both of changing and of staying the same. He tried to be honest, because he knew he wouldn't get better by minimizing the minuses of changing or overemphasizing the pluses of staying the same.

Sample Exercise 3.1 Roman's Pluses and Minuses Worksheet

	Pluses (Benefits)	**Minuses (Costs)**
Change:	*I'll sleep better.* *I won't worry so much about having a panic attack.* *I will be able to keep my job and expand my role in the firm.* *I'll feel better about myself if I overcome my panic disorder.*	*What if I have even more panic attacks?* *Maybe I'll discover that I can't overcome my panic disorder.* *This is going to be hard work, and I barely have time to keep up with my job.*
Staying the Same:	*It's easier not to face my fear.* *Maybe I'm not cut out for law. I could just quit my job and feel much better right away.* *Some days, it's not so bad. Maybe this whole thing will go away on its own.*	*My world will get smaller and smaller.* *I won't be able to move up in the firm, because I'm too anxious.* *I'll become more and more dependent on my wife, which will really mess up our relationship.*

Now, you try. Take your time and think through all the pluses and minuses of changing and of staying the same. This exercise is for you, so be honest. The choice of whether or not to begin your recovery is yours.

Exercise 3.1 Pluses and Minuses Worksheet

	Pluses (Benefits)	Minuses (Costs)
Change:		
Staying the Same:		

SECOND LOOK AT YOUR PLUSES AND MINUSES

You might have focused on one side of the equation—the minuses of change and pluses of staying the same—for so long that you have developed tunnel vision. Even though you want to see the other side of the equation, it might be difficult for you. The following exercise might help you open your lens a little more so that change seems not only possible, but also desirable. Imagine inviting a trusted friend or relative to counter your minuses of changing and pluses of staying the same. Imagine how your friend might challenge your assumptions in a noncritical and caring way. How would your friend answer the following questions? *What is a different view of this point? Are there new opportunities you're missing? Are there different possibilities to consider? Is there another way to look at this point that would enhance your motivation? Is there a way to alter a minus of changing or plus of staying the same that encourages you to try?*

Roman completed the following exercise easily. He imagined that he was the defense attorney in the case against his recovery and challenged the points made by the prosecuting attorney.

Sample Exercise 3.2 Roman's Second Look at the Pluses and Minuses Worksheet

	Minuses (Costs)	Counterpoint
Change:	*What if I have even more panic attacks?*	*Everything I've read in this book so far tells me that I'm likely to have fewer panic attacks, not more.*
	Maybe I'll discover that I can't overcome my panic disorder.	*Everything I've read so far tells me that the skills in this book work for most people. Why would I be any different?*
	This is going to be hard work, and I barely have time to keep up with my job.	*I'm working really hard right now to keep from having a panic attack. What will my life look like when I don't have to work so hard to prevent panic attacks? I'll be less worried. I'll be able to do more things. I'll be able to put the energy I'm putting into preventing a panic attack into doing more in my job.*

	Pluses (Pros)	Counterpoint
Staying the Same:	*It's easier not to face my fear.*	*I'm working really hard now to stay the same. Yes, I may be more anxious at first, but I can see how I could become less anxious over time.*
	Maybe I'm not cut out for law. I could just quit my job and feel much better right away.	*I love law. Quitting my job doesn't solve this problem, because no matter where you go, there you are. In fact, if I quit my job, I'd probably worry even more about money and finding another job.*
	Some days, it's not so bad. Maybe this whole thing will go away on its own.	*I've been struggling with these symptoms for months now. I've cut back on my work and stress level, but my anxiety is still really high. If it were going to disappear on its own, it should have happened by now. Everything I've read so far about panic disorder tells me it gets worse, not better, if you don't work on it.*

Now, use the following worksheet to take a second look at your pluses and minuses for changing and for staying the same. Take your time and carefully build your counterpoints, or arguments against the minuses of changing and pluses of staying the same. This second look might open your eyes to the real and lasting advantages of moving forward with your recovery.

Exercise 3.2 Second Look at the Pluses and Minuses Worksheet

	Minuses (Costs)	Counterpoint
Change:		
	Pluses (Pros)	**Counterpoint**
Staying the Same:		

You've now examined the pluses and minuses of both changing and staying the same. Furthermore, you've challenged your pluses of staying the same and minuses of change, and you've a new point of view for your recovery. However, you might need more to motivate yourself than these pluses and minuses. You might require deeper reasons to change. Let's look at what motivates us to change, particularly in deep and personal ways—our values.

LET YOUR VALUES LEAD THE WAY

Your values give meaning to your life. They inspire, motivate, and nurture you. Your values direct you in life and represent what you want your life to be about in a deep and personal way. Additionally, your values motivate deep change, such as breaking free from anxiety and avoidance to live a fuller and more vital life. Values also help you see beyond those anxious moments that can prevent you from doing what you really want to do, and would do if you weren't focused on avoiding that moment of anxiety or fear. In this section, you'll learn the importance of connecting with your values and letting them lead you toward a fuller, less anxious, and more meaningful life (Eifert and Forsyth 2005).

Self-Assessment: A Look at Your Values

Values are not the same as goals (Hayes, Strosahl, and Wilson 1999). Values are a direction, or course (for example, sailing south along the California coast), and goals are specific destinations, or points (San Francisco, Santa Barbara, Los Angeles, San Diego), along the way as you move in the direction of a given value. Values are a process, and goals are a product. Integrity is a value, and speaking truthfully and sensitively to colleagues and friends is a goal. Health is a value, and meeting yearly with your physician is a goal. Values aren't desires, wishes, or preferences, such as sex, more money, or Indian food. Values are truths, beliefs, or understandings. Some values, like charity or generosity, are in the service of others. Other values, like creativity or spirituality, are most often in the service of your own welfare and growth.

DEFINING CORE VALUES

Ten domains capture the most important core values that motivate us to strive and change (Hayes, Strosahl, and Wilson 1999). These domains cover common areas of life for most people. You'll find that some of the values in the following list are very important to you, and others less so.

Family. This domain is about the importance of your relationships with your immediate family. Through this value, you learn to love. You also find support and acceptance that stabilizes your life and is the springboard to loving others. Terms for values in the domain of family are "love," "acceptance," and "respect." Does your anxiety create distress or resentment in your relationships with family members? Are you overly dependent on your parents? Are you too anxious to speak your mind, resulting in relationships that aren't as honest and truthful as you would like?

Intimate relationships. This domain is about your relationship with your significant other: spouse, partner, lover, boyfriend, or girlfriend. Through this value, you deepen your capacity to love and accept love. You learn to trust and honor a special person. If you aren't with someone now, you can still connect with this domain by working toward an ideal future relationship. Terms for values in the domain of intimate relationships are "fidelity," "openness," and "love." Because of your anxiety, do you avoid physical intimacy with your spouse or significant other? Do you worry excessively that your partner will leave you at any moment? Are you too anxious to ask out a special person or to say yes when a special person asks you out?

Parenting. This domain is about your life as a parent. If you can't have children, or can but don't have children currently, you can still connect with this domain by working toward becoming a "parent" to some future child or young adult. Through this value, you connect to the teacher and protector in you. You learn to love another without expectation that the other will always return it in equal measure. You can share the wisdom you've gained in living your life with meaning and integrity. Terms for values in the domain of parenting are "love," "protect," and "teach." Are you too anxious to set limits with your children that will help them become responsible and caring adults? Does your anxiety cause you to overprotect your children, thereby denying them the experiences that will make them stronger and more capable? Do you want children but are too afraid to try?

Friends and social life. This domain is about the importance of friendships and having a full and vibrant social life. Through this value, you build a supportive friendship network. You nurture caring and loyal friends. You live fully as a social being. Terms for values in the domain of friends and social life are "love," "loyalty," and "trust." Does your anxiety cause you to spend too much time alone? Do you decline invitations to go out with friends because you're too worried or anxious? Do your "friends" treat you poorly, but you're too anxious to find new ones?

Work and career. This domain is about bringing integrity, passion, and excellence to your work life. Through this value, you take on professional challenges that excite you and advance your career. You earn the respect of your supervisors and coworkers. You learn the importance of working hard for something that you believe will make a positive difference for you and others. Terms for values in the domain of work and career are "excellence," "stewardship," and "professionalism." Are you too afraid to take on new challenges at work? Are you so worried that your boss will fire you or that your coworkers will dislike you that you don't speak your mind? Are you too anxious to take advantage of the opportunities at work that attracted you to the job in the first place?

Education and learning. This domain is about learning and discovery. Through this value, you connect to the thrill and excitement of learning something new. You seek truth and wisdom. Terms for values in the domain of education and learning are "truth," "wisdom," and "skill." Did you attend a college that wasn't your first choice, because you were too anxious to attend one farther from home? Are you a lifelong learner, but afraid to take a class? Does your anxiety prevent you from speaking to your teachers or participating fully in class discussions?

Recreation and leisure. This domain is about seeking balance between work and play. Through this value, you connect to the child in you. You recharge and reconnect with family and friends. You learn to appreciate the quiet moments that punctuate life and give it rhythm and meaning. Terms for values in the domain of recreation and leisure are "creativity," "fun," and "passion." Are you too anxious to set limits with a supervisor who keeps giving you too much work, such that you don't have time for fun? Do you worry excessively even when you're on vacation or playing a sport? Does your anxiety wear you down and deplete your energy to have fun with a sport or activity?

Spirituality and faith. This domain is about connecting to something larger than you are. Through this value, you learn the importance of believing in something you can't see or touch. You connect with the arc of life: its beginning and end. Spirituality takes many forms. For one person, spirituality might mean attending services within an organized religion. For another, spirituality might mean meditating or taking long walks in the woods alone to connect with nature or to collect your thoughts. Terms for values in the domain of spirituality and faith are "God," "faith," "higher power," and "the universe." Does your anxiety make it difficult for you to find the inner peace that means "spirituality" to you? Are you too fearful to attend services at your church, mosque, or temple? Do you worry so much about what others think about you that you don't seek the wisdom and advice of your priest, rabbi, or other faith leader?

Community life and citizenship. This domain is about service and responsibility to others. Through this value, you contribute to bettering the world and your place in it somehow. Terms for values in the domain of community life and citizenship are "justice," "responsibility," and "charity." Does your anxiety keep you from taking on charitable work or political action? Do you avoid serving your community or participating in your neighborhood life?

Health and self-care. This domain is about taking care of your physical health. Through this value, you connect with your life force. You get the most out of each day and each task, because you're healthy, vital, and nourished. Terms for values in the domain of health and self-care are "health," "strength," and "vitality." Because of your anxiety, do you avoid routine medical or dental care? Does your anxiety cause you to avoid joining a gym or health club? Does it cause you to eat too much or too little?

IDENTIFYING CORE VALUES

Identifying core values is a process of reflection and discovery. Few of us take the time to identify what is truly important to us. This is not to say that your values are not guiding and motivating you. If you're passionate about something, whether it's basketball or running for political office, a core value is likely leading the way. Remember Bart, the chemistry graduate student with obsessive-compulsive disorder? Bart's contamination obsessions terrify him, and the idea of facing his fears, even step by step, terrifies him too. Bart will need to connect to his values in order to progress in his recovery. Bart's health is suffering, and he might not graduate if he doesn't get a handle on his obsessive-compulsive symptoms. Furthermore, Bart is spending so much time washing and cleaning that he has little time to connect with friends and family. Look at part I of Bart's Valued Living Questionnaire (sample exercise 3.3). The values that are most important to Bart center on family, friends, work, and education. Remember, there are no right or wrong answers. Bart values what he values; these values are unique to him and may differ greatly from the values you identify as important to you.

Next, Bart completed part II of the Valued Living Questionnaire and rated how consistent he had been during the last week with putting his values into action. This was difficult for Bart, because he wanted to mark how he thought he "should" act rather than how he really behaved. Nevertheless, Bart answered honestly, because he realized that to recover from his OCD, it was essential that he understand how his anxious response was holding him back from living in accordance with his important personal values.

Sample Exercise 3.3 Bart's Valued Living Questionnaire

Your Values: Part I

Instructions: Begin the Valued Living Questionnaire with an assessment of your current values. People value some areas of life more than other areas. The value, or importance, that you place on different areas of living is unique to you. There are no right or wrong answers here.

Rate the importance of each area (by circling a number) on a scale from 1 to 10, where 1 means that the area is not at all important to you and 10 means that the area is very important to you. You may not value all these areas or value all areas the same.

Area	Not at all important								Extremely important	
1. Family (other than marriage or parenting)	1	2	3	4	5	6	7	**(8)**	9	10
2. Intimate relationships	1	2	**(3)**	4	5	6	7	8	**9**	10
3. Parenting	**(1)**	2	3	4	5	6	7	8	9	10
4. Friends and social life	1	2	3	4	5	6	7	8	**(9)**	10
5. Work and career	1	2	3	4	5	6	7	8	**(9)**	10
6. Education and learning	1	2	3	4	5	6	7	8	**(9)**	10
7. Recreation and leisure	1	2	3	4	**(5)**	6	7	8	9	10
8. Spirituality and faith	**(1)**	2	3	4	5	6	7	8	9	10
9. Community life and citizenship	1	2	**(3)**	4	5	6	7	8	9	10
10. Health and self-care (diet, exercise, sleep)	1	2	3	4	**(5)**	6	7	8	9	10

Your Values: Part II		
During the past week		
Area	**Not at all consistent with my value**	**Completely consistent with my value**
1. Family (other than marriage or parenting)	1 (2) 3 4 5 6 7 8 9 10	
2 Intimate relationships	1 (2) 3 4 5 6 7 8 9 10	
3. Parenting	1 2 3 4 5 6 7 8 9 (10)	
4. Friends and social life	1 (2) 3 4 5 6 7 8 9 10	
5. Work and career	1 2 (3) 4 5 6 7 8 9 10	
6. Education and learning	1 2 (3) 4 5 6 7 8 9 10	
7. Recreation and leisure	1 2 (3) 4 5 6 7 8 9 10	
8. Spirituality and faith	1 2 3 4 5 6 7 8 9 (10)	
9. Community life and citizenship	1 2 3 4 5 6 7 8 (9) 10	
10. Health and self-care (diet, exercise, sleep)	1 (2) 3 4 5 6 7 8 9 10	

Now, complete your own Valued Living Questionnaire. For part I read the list of the ten domains of core values. Do any of these domains speak to you? Consider each domain carefully and ask yourself how important it is to you. Circle the number on the scale (from 1, "Not at all important," to 10, "Extremely important").

For part II, rate how consistent your actions have been during the past week with each of your values. Remember, rate your actions honestly, and don't rate them based on how you or others believe you "should" have, or wish you had, acted.

Exercise 3.3 Valued Living Questionnaire

Your Values: Part I

Instructions: Begin the Valued Living Questionnaire with an assessment of your current values. People value some areas of life more than other areas. The value, or importance, that you place on different areas of living is unique to you. There are no right or wrong answers here.

Rate the importance of each area (by circling a number) on a scale from 1 to 10, where 1 means that the area is not at all important to you and 10 means that the area is very important to you. You may not value all these areas or value all areas the same.

Area	Not at all important								Extremely important
1. Family (other than marriage or parenting)	1	2	3	4	5	6	7	8	9	10
2. Intimate relationships	1	2	3	4	5	6	7	8	9	10
3. Parenting	1	2	3	4	5	6	7	8	9	10
4. Friends and social life	1	2	3	4	5	6	7	8	9	10
5. Work and career	1	2	3	4	5	6	7	8	9	10
6. Education and learning	1	2	3	4	5	6	7	8	9	10
7. Recreation and leisure	1	2	3	4	5	6	7	8	9	10
8. Spirituality and faith	1	2	3	4	5	6	7	8	9	10
9. Community life and citizenship	1	2	3	4	5	6	7	8	9	10
10. Health and self-care (diet, exercise, sleep)	1	2	3	4	5	6	7	8	9	10

Your Values: Part II		
During the past week		
Area	**Not at all consistent with my value**	**Completely consistent with my value**
1. Family (other than marriage or parenting)	1 2 3 4 5 6 7 8	9 10
2 Intimate relationships	1 2 3 4 5 6 7 8	9 10
3. Parenting	1 2 3 4 5 6 7 8	9 10
4. Friends and social life	1 2 3 4 5 6 7 8	9 10
5. Work and career	1 2 3 4 5 6 7 8	9 10
6. Education and learning	1 2 3 4 5 6 7 8	9 10
7. Recreation and leisure	1 2 3 4 5 6 7 8	9 10
8. Spirituality and faith	1 2 3 4 5 6 7 8	9 10
9. Community life and citizenship	1 2 3 4 5 6 7 8	9 10
10. Health and self-care (diet, exercise, sleep)	1 2 3 4 5 6 7 8	9 10

Values in Action

The objective of the values assessment you just completed is to connect you to the important personal values that can motivate you to advance your recovery and keep it moving during the inevitable difficult points along the way. Now, let's translate your values into action. Values in action are committed actions (Hayes, Strosahl, and Wilson 1999; Hayes 2005)— that is, a *willingness* on your part to feel anxiety, fear, and distress in the service of your values. Through willingness, you make what seems unbearable a bit more bearable. Through willingness, you gain some influence over how you feel and what you do. Through willingness, you take control of your recovery.

Moving forward means that you're willing to face the discomfort, anxiety, and fear that are part of any recovery from excessive anxiety or an anxiety disorder. Willingness is a choice, and you've learned strategies to help you choose: decisional analysis and values clarification. In addition, you've learned about the nature of motivation, including some factors that can increase or decrease it. Furthermore, you've learned the central role that motivation will play in your recovery and the importance of drinking frequently from the well of motivation in order to persevere.

The next chapter presents *disengaged awareness*, the act of watching and waiting rather than avoiding and reacting. You'll learn the benefits of watching and waiting, plus several watching and waiting strategies.

CHAPTER 4

Watching and Waiting

As you've learned, your secondary anxious response (SAR) to what is a normal and natural initial experience is why you suffer. This SAR is the way in which you interpret, evaluate, or appraise your primary, or initial, anxious response, and this SAR causes you to feel even more anxious and for longer than is helpful. By now, you've learned the three parts of this SAR—anxious mind, anxious body, and anxious actions. However, even when you know the parts, it's not easy to break your anxious response apart when you're feeling anxious or afraid. There's something about anxiety and fear that makes it difficult to watch and wait long enough to break apart our anxious response, even when we're willing to try.

In this chapter, you'll learn to watch your secondary anxious response in a different way. Watching and waiting is an essential skill to help you manage your secondary anxious responses. Watching and waiting is the basis of much that follows in this book, particularly as you learn to step toward discomfort to overcome your fears and the avoidance that holds you back. Let's start by defining watching and waiting—present-focused and nonjudgmental awareness, or mindfulness—and then explore the reasons why watching and waiting can help you recover from your excessive anxiety or anxiety disorder. Later, you'll find several exercises to help you learn to watch and wait, including ways to anchor yourself in the present, the heart of watching and waiting.

WATCHING YOUR ANXIOUS RESPONSE

You're probably already watching your secondary anxious response. In fact, you might be keenly aware of it and wish you could be less aware of it. However, even though you're aware of your anxious responses, you're not necessarily watching them in a helpful way.

If you're watching your secondary anxious responses in a helpful way, you're watching in two ways: You're watching your anxious response without judgment about value or worth, and you're watching your anxious response in the present moment, as it is happening now. Watching and waiting in this way involves focusing your attention on the present moment rather than on the future or the past. Watching and waiting is seeing, hearing, and feeling what's happening now. As you watch and wait, you're less likely to get caught up in the "what ifs" of the future: *What if I have a panic attack? What if the dog bites me? What if she thinks I'm weird?* When you watch and wait in this way, you swim in the river of now: your ongoing experience of what's happening in your mind, your body, and the space around you. This form of watching and waiting is present-focused and nonjudgmental awareness, or mindfulness.

BENEFITS OF BEING HERE, NOT THERE

Now, when you watch your secondary anxious response, you likely do so in a way that causes you to feel overwhelmed by your anxiety. Your anxious responses might confuse you. They might seem to "happen" automatically or come out of nowhere. You might watch your anxious response with the hope of controlling it, only to learn that when you watch in this way, you feel more out of control of it.

When you watch and wait—mindfully—you step out of the cycle of interacting with thoughts, feelings, and actions in order to see things as they really are. Once you step away from your secondary anxious response, you can truly see whether it accurately reflects the situation you're in right now. Are you really in danger or not, right now? For example, if you have panic disorder and worry that the tight feeling in your chest means that you're suffocating and dying, pulling back to the present moment can help. Ask yourself, *Am I still breathing at this moment? Am I still alive at this moment?* You can answer that question clearly and accurately only in the present moment.

Because this form of watching and waiting is rooted in the present, you react less often, as a result of learning something about your anxious response. You watch your anxiety rise, crest, and decrease again, rather than watch what you fear—that it will build and build without end. Watching and waiting in this way helps counteract your worries about your anxious response, that this experience will go on forever and that there's no end to how bad it might get. Watching and waiting will help you learn that you have nothing to fear from your secondary anxious response, that it's a small part of your experience, one that you can manage and even learn to value.

Last, as you learn to watch and wait, you develop a skill that helps you resist the urge to avoid, to escape from, or to neutralize—these are the anxious actions that create so many problems for you. Similarly, as you learn to watch and wait, you uncover an alternative to suppressing your anxious response or distracting yourself from it, other maladaptive ways of responding to anxiety that fuel the problem. Watching and waiting—mindfully—places your anxiety in context. Your anxious experiences are just one piece of any present moment that includes many other pieces: what you see, touch, and hear. In other words, your anxious experience is an important piece of your experience in a particular moment, but not necessarily the most important aspect of your total experience of being in the world.

LEARNING TO WATCH AND WAIT

Learning to watch and wait—that is, to be mindfully aware of the present moment—doesn't come naturally to us. Our minds don't work that way. Our minds, by nature, take us into the future or back to the past, which is a helpful tendency. Our minds' ability to anticipate problems or threats protects us from the real dangers and difficulties we face in our lives. Our minds' ability to revisit the past helps us learn what worked or didn't work so that we can be more effective and prepared in the present. Learning to watch and wait—to pay attention to your anxious response in the present moment and to observe it objectively, nonjudgmentally, and with acceptance and understanding—takes time and practice. It's not an easy skill to learn, because in a sense, you're working against your mind's natural tendency to move away from the present. However, it's a skill that you can develop and one that you'll use throughout your recovery from your excessive anxiety or anxiety disorder.

The first step in learning to watch and wait is to try out this new attitude of observing your experience as it occurs in the present moment. If you have an anxiety disorder, you might have spent many years dwelling on the future, among all the "what ifs," and the present moment might be foreign territory. The following exercises introduce you to the experience of watching and waiting. Set aside about five minutes each day to practice one of the next two exercises.

Exercise 4.1 Inside and Outside

This exercise is a great introduction to watching and waiting, because you learn to distinguish between experiences happening inside your mind and body and experiences happening in the outside world.

Close your eyes and take a deep breath. Gently move your attention to your body. Observe any pleasant sensations or feelings. If you notice pain or tension, observe that too, but don't linger there. Perhaps you notice other sensations: heat, cold, or pressure on a part of your body. Notice the feeling of the floor beneath your feet and your weight in the chair if you're sitting. Notice your breath: the gentle rise and fall of your abdomen, or the movement of air in and out of your nostrils.

After a minute or two of looking inside your mind and body, open your eyes and shift your attention to the environment around you. What do you see, hear, and smell? What do you feel: the texture and weight of your clothing or the temperature of the air around you? Just move from one sense to another: sight, sound, smell, taste, and touch. Let your attention drift to sounds: the soft ticking of a clock or the hum of the air conditioner. Let your attention focus on colors and shapes around you: the pattern in the carpet or the shape of a doorknob. Let your attention wander farther, perhaps outside the room or building, to notice other sounds: a honking car horn or the sound of a door opening or closing.

After a minute or two of looking outside your mind and body, close your eyes and shift your attention back to the inside. Open your attention to other sensations—those that you missed before—throughout your body, noticing what you feel. Again, if you notice anything uncomfortable or unpleasant, rest your attention there for just a moment and move on to whatever else there is to notice. After a minute or two, open your eyes and shift your attention back to the outside one more time.

At the end of the exercise, take a few moments to reflect on and record your experiences using the following worksheet. What did you notice in your inner and outer worlds? In which world were you most comfortable and at peace? In which world was your mind most quiet? In which world was your mind most active? Did you judge your experience? Did you think *That's a dumb thought* or *That's a weird feeling.* Did you feel frustrated with yourself and think, *What's my problem?* I should be better at this!

Tyra tried this exercise and discovered that sometimes she felt relaxed and at ease, and other times she felt frustrated and anxious. Interestingly, Tyra learned that she was most at ease when she paid attention to her senses, and she was most frustrated and anxious when she paid attention to her thoughts.

Tyra's Watching and Waiting Worksheet

	Inner World — What did you notice about your mind (thoughts, images), body (physical sensations), and actions (behaviors)?			Outer World — What did you notice about the environment around you (sights, sounds, smells)?	Did You Judge Your Experience? 0 (not at all)–10 (very much)
	Mind	Body	Actions		
Sunday	I can't focus. What if I never find a job?	I feel tense and have a headache. I couldn't eat much today.	I kept looking at the clock and tried to relax my shoulders.	I heard birds chirping outside.	5
Monday	I noticed the doubts about finding a job again.	More tension, especially around my eyes.	I changed positions.	I focused on the sounds of my boyfriend making lunch.	3
Tuesday	I noticed my "put-down" thoughts.	Tense, restless.	I focused on my breath.	I smelled smoke from the grill next door.	6
Wednesday	I'm not doing this right. I'm such a loser.	Frustrated and tense.	I focused on the feeling of cool air coming into my nostrils.	I focused on the sound of the fan in the next room.	8
Thursday					
Friday					
Saturday					

Watching and Waiting Worksheet

	Inner World What did you notice about your mind (thoughts, images), body (physical sensations), and actions (behaviors)?			Outer World What did you notice about the environment around you (sights, sounds, smells)?	Did You Judge Your Experience? 0 (not at all)–10 (very much)
	Mind	Body	Actions		
Sunday					
Monday					
Tuesday					
Wednesday					
Thursday					
Friday					
Saturday					

Exercise 4.2 Mindfulness of Your Emotions

When you feel anxious, you can learn to watch your anxious response mindfully so that the feeling doesn't carry you away. To learn to watch and wait in this way, you can practice this exercise for any emotion: anxiety, frustration, guilt, or sadness. Just watch the feeling and label it. Watch the feeling as if that emotion were completely new to you. Observe its shades. Observe the ups and downs and the qualities of the entire experience. Try to describe the feeling as fully as possible, as if you were a scientist trying to record this new experience.

Don't try to suppress or distract yourself from the feeling. Let it be whatever it is and as strong as it is. Don't judge the feeling or yourself for having it. As you observe a feeling, you'll notice *action urges*: an impetus to do something. Every feeling has an action urge. For example, anger typically makes you want to strike out. If the feeling is anxiety, you might feel the urge to escape, avoid, or neutralize your anxious response. These urges signal that your anxious actions are knocking at the door. Just watch these urges without acting on them. Just watch the feeling, and wait. Watch and wait. Here's how to do this:

1. Acknowledge and label the feeling. Observe it briefly to see how strong it is and whether other emotions (anxiety, anger, guilt, shame, sadness) are mixed in.

2. Observe your breath. Bring your attention to your abdomen as you breathe in and out.

3. When thoughts arise, greet them and then let them go. Say, *Hello thought,* or *Thank you, mind, for that thought.* Return your attention to your breath as you observe other parts of the feeling.

4. Open your awareness, like the lens of a camera, so that you become more conscious of the space around you. Watch for other emotions, for sensations in your body, and the sights, sounds, and smells outside your body. Then move your awareness beyond the room you're in (for example) to the building, to the neighborhood, to the town in which you live.

5. Watch and wait, and as you do this, observe the feeling in the context of your body within the larger world around you.

6. Continue to watch and wait until the feeling subsides, as waves do; until the feeling changes into another feeling; or until you've practiced enough.

The point of watching a feeling—particularly your anxious response—is to learn to let the feeling be what it is. If you have been anxious for many years, you likely have developed a push-away attitude toward your anxious response. Learning to watch and wait helps you develop a new attitude toward it. Rather than running away from your anxious response, you learn to turn toward it and watch it rise and fall like a wave. You learn the power of turning toward your anxious response in the present moment with openness and acceptance. Now, you try it.

WAYS TO ANCHOR YOURSELF HERE, NOT THERE

Now that you've introduced yourself to the act of watching an emotion in a present-focused, non-judgmental way, you might have noticed something: It's not easy to stay in the present moment. Our minds tend to swing us away from the present moment unless we have an anchor. As you'll learn, anything can serve as an anchor: your breath, an activity, or even a word. But be careful how you use your anchor. Don't use your anchor to run away or distract yourself from your anxious response. That's just more of the problem. Instead, the anchor is to guide your attention and awareness back to the present moment when you're feeling anxious. Once you're in the present moment, check in with the parts of your secondary anxious response: anxious mind, anxious body, and anxious actions. Once you're aware of your anxious response in this way, you can more easily determine whether it's an accurate reflection of what's going on at that specific moment. Later, you'll learn different skills to use during these moments to bring your anxious response back on course. For now, the goal is to learn—and learn well—to observe your anxious response in a mindful way.

The Breath as an Anchor

Perhaps there's no better anchor to the present moment than your breath. No matter where you go, there you are and there it is. If you meditate, you know the value of the breath as an anchor to the present moment. Breathing mindfully invites feelings of peace and acceptance. As you accept your feelings, you no longer fight them, and as counterintuitive as this feels, it works. Accepting whatever is happening in the moment—including whatever you're feeling—is a powerful way to quiet your secondary anxious response.

When you breathe mindfully, you attend to your breath without judgment. To attend to your breath, anchor your attention on some part of your body that the breath touches. You might observe the feel of the air coming through your nose or mouth, the rise and fall of your abdomen, or the way your ribs expand and contract with each breath in and out. Once you have anchored yourself in the present moment through attention to the breath, you can notice and let go of each thought that enters your awareness. You acknowledge the thought (perhaps by saying gently to yourself, *Thought*) and return your attention to your breath. As you practice breathing mindfully, you'll notice your attention wandering away from your breath to greet thoughts. Don't feel discouraged or frustrated by this. This is normal and natural. Our minds naturally distract us from what we're doing. Even people who have meditated for many years find that their minds wander. Perhaps through practice, you'll learn to rest your attention a bit more on your breath than your thoughts, but you'll never be able to lock your attention on the breath so that it never moves back to your thoughts. That's not possible for anyone. Furthermore, you'll never be able to get rid of an unwanted thought. In fact, that's not the goal of mindfulness. The goal of mindfulness is to change the way you relate to your thoughts. Instead of struggling with your thoughts, you learn to let go of them and return to the present moment. In a sense, you learn to let go of pieces of your secondary anxious response and return to the present moment, thereby calming your body and mind.

Exercise 4.3 Use Your Breath as an Anchor

Here's a simple script to help you learn to anchor yourself in the present moment by breathing mindfully. If you like, record this passage and listen to it as you practice. Practice breathing mindfully three times a day. Start with just 2 minutes of practice each time and add a minute; as you become more comfortable and confident, you can go up to 5 minutes. Once you reach 5 minutes per practice, try bundling these 5-minute practices into a single 15-minute practice. The benefits of these longer periods of mindful breathing can last for many hours, which makes it well worth the time you set aside to do it. To help you remember to practice, link it to something you do every day—for example, make it a habit to practice before showering, before eating, or before returning a phone call.

Close your eyes or fix your eyes on a spot in front of you, and bring your attention to your breathing. Observe your breathing as if you've never encountered breathing before. Observe your breathing as if you're a curious scientist who wishes to observe the process closely, without judgment. Notice the air as it comes into your nostrils and moves down to the bottom of your lungs, and notice the air come back out again. Notice how the air is slightly warmer as it goes out and slightly cooler as it goes in. (Pause for 5 seconds.) *Notice the gentle rise and fall of your shoulders with each breath—and the slow rise and fall of your rib cage—and the comfortable rise and fall of your abdomen.* (Pause for 5 seconds.) *Rest your attention on one of these areas now, whichever you prefer, on the breath moving in and out of your nostrils, on the gentle rise and fall of your shoulders, or on the easy rise and fall of your abdomen. Rest your attention on this spot and notice the in and out of the breath.* (Pause for 10 seconds.)

Whatever feelings, urges, or sensations arise, whether pleasant or unpleasant, gently acknowledge them and let them be. Gently acknowledge them as if you were nodding your head at someone passing by on the street—and return your attention to the breath. (Pause for 10 seconds.) *Whatever thoughts, images, or memories arise, whether comfortable or uncomfortable, gently acknowledge them and let them be. Let them come and go as they please, and return your attention to the breath.* (Pause for 10 seconds.) *From time to time, your attention will wander away from the breath, and each time this happens, notice what distracted you and then bring your attention back to the breath. No matter how often you drift off into your thoughts, whether a hundred times or a thousand, simply note what distracted you and return your attention to the breath.* (Pause for 10 seconds.) *Again and again, your mind will wander away from the breath. This is normal and natural, and it happens to everyone. Our minds naturally distract us from what we're doing, so each time this happens, gently acknowledge it, notice what distracted you, and then return your attention to the breath.* (Pause for 10 seconds.) *If frustration, boredom, anxiety, or other feelings arise, simply acknowledge them and return your attention to the breath.* (Pause for 10 seconds.) *No matter how often your mind wanders, gently acknowledge it, note what distracted you, and return your attention to the breath.*

Daily Activities as an Anchor

Just because you're active and busy doesn't mean you can't be present. Activities—particularly the small ones you do every day—are terrific anchors to the present moment. Doing the dishes, taking a shower, climbing the stairs, walking to the bus stop, eating lunch, and hugging someone you love are examples of the small things we do every day, but perhaps not mindfully. The best activities for present-focused anchors are physical, not mental, activities, so that you can observe every detail of the experience. It doesn't matter what activity you choose, so long as it's brief, you can do it every day, and you can use all your senses (smell, taste, touch, hearing, and vision). For example, as you walk from the front door to the kitchen, focus on the smells of your house. Observe the pattern in the carpet or drapes. Feel the weight of your steps and the sound you make walking across the carpet or floor. Pay attention to where you place your keys or lunch bag, and listen to the sound it makes as you drop it there.

As you practice mindfulness during these activities, observe any thoughts that enter your mind. Notice and label them, and then return your attention to your five senses. As your attention drifts away, gently nudge it back to the sensory details of what you're doing at that moment. You might want to use signs or signals to remind you to act mindfully. If you plan to eat breakfast mindfully, make a paper placemat on which you've written "Mindful." If you plan to walk up the stairs mindfully, place a sign on one of the steps to remind you. If you wish to practice mindfully walking home, pick a house or storefront along the way to serve as your "mindful" spot that reminds you to shift your attention to mindful walking.

Perhaps begin with just a single daily activity and practice it mindfully for a week. Later, add another activity and another. Try to plan activities throughout the day—morning, afternoon, evening—so that you're practicing mindful activities all day long.

"And" Take a Moment to Watch and Wait

Another way to anchor yourself in the present moment is to center on a word or phrase. For example, on your drive to work, you can pick out the word "and" as you listen to song lyrics or to a newscast. As you stand in a crowded restaurant or ride the bus to work, listen for the word "and" in the conversations around you. As you walk to work, notice the "and" on the signs and billboards around you. This simple skill pulls you back to the present moment, and once you're there, you can watch and wait.

Watching and waiting is an important skill that helps you unhook from your secondary anxious response so that you can calm your mind and body. Once you have unhooked in this way, you can observe your situation more clearly and accurately. The power of watching and waiting rests on your ability to return to the present moment, and you've learned several ways to anchor yourself in the present when you're feeling anxious.

The next chapter describes the role that your thinking plays in your secondary anxious response and points out typical thinking traps that fuel it. You'll learn skills to shift your thinking so that you can view the situations that fuel your anxiety in more flexible and reasonable ways. This important skill will loosen the old and rigid beliefs that contribute to your secondary anxious response.

CHAPTER 5

Thinking Inside and Outside the Anxiety Box

When you have an anxiety disorder, your pattern of anxious thinking—a part of your secondary anxious response—has boxed you in. Once you're boxed in by the way you think, it's difficult for you to step outside the anxiety box so that you can see things as they really are. It's the inflexibility of your anxious thinking—rather than the anxious thoughts themselves—that fuels your anxiety and avoidance. The goal, then, is to increase the flexibility of your anxious mind by increasing your ability to shift and change your anxious thoughts when you wish.

In this chapter, you'll learn more about your pattern of anxious thinking—particularly the way you interpret and appraise situations that make you anxious and keep you trapped in the anxiety box. Later in this chapter, you'll learn strategies to step outside your anxiety box so that you can live a more comfortable and fuller life.

INSIDE THE ANXIETY BOX

The anxiety box is any rigid pattern of thinking that makes you anxious and causes you to avoid many things in life. But the pattern isn't the problem; this same pattern protects you when you're in true danger. It's the inflexibility of the pattern that's the problem. You can't step out of the pattern—step outside the anxiety box—when you wish to see to see that the threat isn't likely to happen and isn't as terrible as you might fear. In this section, you'll learn more about your tendency to interpret and predict things in particular ways: how you focus on one interpretation or prediction over another, and the meanings you assign to events and situations that fuel your anxiety and cause you to avoid many things.

Appraisals Include Our Biases and Interpretations

In any given situation or event, you can focus on one aspect of your experience over another. Certain things catch the attention of your anxious mind, and furthermore, it tends to focus on one thing and not another. Your anxious mind latches on to aspects of your experience automatically and quickly. For example, during a piano lesson, your teacher might praise your effort and the way you hit every note with just the right feeling. She might praise you for knowing the piece by heart and for sitting correctly at the piano. She then mentions that you might try holding two notes at the end of a measure a little longer to emphasize the mood you're trying to create. After your lesson, on your drive home, all you can remember is what she said about improving the piece. It's difficult to remember the many good things she said about your playing, if you remember them at all. Our minds tend to work in this way. They focus on one thing over another; they might focus on either praise or criticism, on a frown or a smile, or on the watch a friend is wearing or the color of someone's shoes. These biases can quickly fuel your anxious response.

In addition to focusing on one thing over another, your mind can interpret the event on which it has focused in many ways. For example, you might interpret your piano teacher's feedback as proof that you're a poor student and that she's disappointed in you (for example, *I really blew that song. She must think I'm not trying*), or you might interpret the feedback to mean that your teacher thinks you're a good student and ready to try something more difficult (for example, *I'm making great progress. My teacher thinks I'm ready to take on the next challenge*). Certain interpretations can quickly fuel your anxious response too.

Automatic Appraisals

Our biases and interpretations—our appraisals—are helpful, because they focus our minds on certain aspects of a situation and certain meanings that we've learned. In this way, our minds improve our ability to live in a complicated and fast-paced world. Assigning certain meanings over other meanings enhances our ability to respond quickly and efficiently to the small and large—to the safe and potentially dangerous—things in life. These appraisals are automatic and for that reaso anxiety experts call them automatic appraisals. For example, as you cross the street and hear a car quickly approaching, it's very important that your mind focus on the speed of the car over its color and conclude quickly that this situation is dangerous so that you can step out of the way. This pattern of thinking is part of your primary anxious response. This pattern is helpful even if afterward you realize you weren't in danger, because at the time, you weren't certain whether you were in danger or not.

Over time, however, you can develop a secondary anxious response, and it's this pattern or style of appraising situations or events that can become as automatic and quick as your primary anxious response. This means that you think and react in the same way over and over until it becomes second nature. Because your anxious mind is in a rut, it's difficult to step outside the anxiety box, even when you would like to stop worrying and avoiding the things that make you anxious. The goal, then, is to become a more flexible thinker and to be able to more easily shift your pattern of anxious thinking when you wish.

STEPPING OUTSIDE THE ANXIETY BOX AND LOOKING IN

The first step in developing a more flexible anxious mind is to look inside the anxiety box in which you're trapped to see what you can learn. In this section, you'll learn the thinking patterns that keep you trapped in a cycle of anxiety and avoidance. Additionally, you'll learn strategies to help you think more flexibly—that is, to become an outside-the-box kind of thinker.

Identifying the Hot Thought

Your pattern of anxious thinking likely includes many different automatic appraisals, but not all appraisals are the same. Some appraisals cause you to feel more anxious than others, partly because some appraisals have scarier meanings than others do. The scariest appraisal—that is, the appraisal that's at the heart of your anxious response—is the *hot appraisal* or *hot thought*. It's essential that you learn to identify the hot thought that drives your anxious response. Once you identify the hot thought, you'll be able to effectively examine whether your anxious response makes sense, given the situation.

The "downward arrow" technique is a simple strategy that you can use to identify your hot anxious thought (Burns 1980). To identify your hot thought, look at a few of your ARC Worksheets (see exercise 2.1). Write your anxious thought (automatic appraisal) on the first line of the Identify Your Hot Thought Worksheet (exercise 5.1), and then ask yourself several questions: *If this were true, what would this mean about me* (or *other people*)? *What would happen if this were true? What would happen next? Why does this matter to me?* Then, answer the question most directly linked to the anxious thought. For example, for Rosey's anxious thought, *What if he sees that I'm blushing* (see sample exercise 5.1), she asked herself, *What would happen if this (he sees me blushing) were true?* and answered, *He'll think I'm weird.* To that appraisal, Rosey asked herself, *What would happen next?* and answered, *If he thinks I'm weird, then he'll tell all the other teachers and staff.* This is a bit like peeling an onion, where one anxious thought or automatic appraisal lies just beneath the one above. In a few steps, Rosey identified her hot anxious thought, which seemed to be an extreme reaction to her fear of blushing when giving a presentation.

Sample Exercise 5.1 Rosey's Identify Your Hot Thought Worksheet

Automatic appraisal: *What if he sees that I'm blushing?*

> If this were true, what would this mean about me (or other people)?
> *What would happen if this were true?*
> What would happen next? Why does this matter to me?

Underlying appraisal: *He'll think I'm weird.*

> If this were true, what would this mean about me (or other people)?
> *What would happen if this were true?*
> What would happen next? Why does this matter to me?

Underlying appraisal: *If he thinks I'm weird, he'll tell all the other teachers.*

> If this were true, what would this mean about me (or other people)?
> *What would happen if this were true?*
> What would happen next? Why does this matter to me?

Underlying appraisal: *I'll feel humiliated and have to quit my job.*

> If this were true, what would this mean about me (or other people)?
> *What would happen if this were true?*
> What would happen next? Why does this matter to me?

Underlying appraisal: *I'll never find another job I love, and I'll be miserable for the rest of my life.*

As you'll see, your initial automatic appraisal usually tells only part of the story. As you peel back its layers and get to the hot thought, you'll understand why you feel so anxious. Now, any time you feel overly anxious or are doing one of your anxious actions, particularly when you're avoiding an object or situation that makes you anxious, try to identify your hot anxious thought.

Exercise 5.1 Identify Your Hot Thought Worksheet

Automatic appraisal: _____

If this were true, what would this mean about me (or other people)?
What would happen if this were true?
What would happen next? Why does this matter to me?

Underlying appraisal: _____

If this were true, what would this mean about me (or other people)?
What would happen if this were true?
What would happen next? Why does this matter to me?

Underlying appraisal: _____

If this were true, what would this mean about me (or other people)?
What would happen if this were true?
What would happen next? Why does this matter to me?

Underlying appraisal: _____

If this were true, what would this mean about me (or other people)?
What would happen if this were true?
What would happen next? Why does this matter to me?

Underlying appraisal: _____

If this were true, what would this mean about me (or other people)?
What would happen if this were true?
What would happen next? Why does this matter to me?

Thinking That Keeps You Trapped inside the Anxiety Box

Thinking traps are rigid patterns of thinking that keep you inside the anxiety box. A thinking trap is a tendency to interpret events in a particular way, such that it's difficult to think about an event in any other way. Once you're inside the anxiety box, you feel more and more anxious, and it's more and more difficult to step outside the box to look at things in a different way. Thinking traps are like ruts in the road, worn deep through years of interpreting things in a certain way, and it's not always easy to steer out of a rut, even when you want to. These mental habits form over many years of thinking, feeling, and doing the same thing over and over.

The three most common thinking traps that keep people in the anxiety box are jumping to conclusions, overfocusing on the conclusions that make them anxious, and thinking the worst. Another thinking trap that some people with anxiety disorders have fallen into is the tyranny of "shoulds," which only makes things worse for people who are struggling to manage their anxious responses.

JUMPING TO CONCLUSIONS

When you jump to conclusions, you overestimate the likelihood that something bad will happen, such as that you will contract an illness, fail a test, or die from a panic attack. When the threat or danger is real, this is a very helpful pattern of thinking, because it prepares you to deal with the threat or perhaps even to avoid the danger. This is your anxious mind at its best. However, this pattern of thinking becomes a thinking trap when you're not able to quickly and easily step out of this pattern of thinking to see things as they really are. When you can't step out of this thinking trap, you repeatedly predict bad things that don't occur, and so you feel anxious and frightened for no good reason. For example, Rosey persistently jumps to the conclusion that people can see when she's blushing, without any evidence that her blushing is noticeable to others. Rosey fails to see that just because she feels as if she's blushing doesn't mean that her blushing is as apparent to others as it feels.

OVERFOCUSING ON THE CONCLUSIONS

If the pattern of jumping to conclusions isn't enough to make you needlessly anxious, you might then also overfocus on these anxious conclusions. For example, when Rosey jumps to the conclusion that people will notice that she's blushing, she focuses on that particular conclusion or interpretation, rather than looking around for other explanations or interpretations (for example, *People don't appear to notice that I'm blushing at all*). This pattern of thinking traps Rosey into interpreting or seeing things in a certain way. Furthermore, when Rosey overfocuses on one interpretation, it might not even occur to her that there might be other ways to think about the event or situation. In over-focusing on a certain conclusion, Rosey might not see the evidence that counters the conclusion that makes her anxious: People speak to her. They smile at her. Most important, they almost never ask if she's feeling okay, which would be a natural question if someone saw that Rosey's face looked flushed. The more time you spend focusing on a scary conclusion that's possible but not likely—

rather than on the likely but not-so-scary conclusion—the more you'll feel anxious, engage in anxious actions, and suffer.

THINKING THE WORST, OR CATASTROPHIZING

This thinking trap is the tendency to overestimate not only the likelihood that something bad will happen, but also its impact. Thinking the worst means that your anxious mind tends to jump to the worst conclusion you can imagine; your anxious mind *catastrophizes*. In other words, when the bad thing happens—and you believe it surely will—it will be horrible. For example, Rosey might believe that people who see that she's blushing will think she's weird and treat her with contempt. She might believe that if she blushes—and she believes that she surely will—her principal will fire her, because he believes she's incompetent. Thinking the worst means Rosey believes that the worst will happen even though a much less disastrous outcome is more likely.

Furthermore, when you think the worst, you might also believe that you can't handle it. If you fail a test, you might believe that you'll never recover from this setback. If you have a panic attack, you might believe that the intense and frightening sensations will overwhelm you. We all experience setbacks. We all make mistakes, and bad things do happen. Most of the time, we're able to cope with these things. However, when you underestimate your ability to cope, even a little thing can become a catastrophe—at least in your anxious mind. Tyra's belief that she couldn't cope with losing Pete, her boyfriend, makes it difficult for her to enjoy her time with him. Although Tyra and Pete get along well, relationships do end, and believing that she couldn't cope with the loss only makes something that would be difficult into something that would be truly catastrophic.

THE TYRANNY OF "SHOULDS"

It's important to have *principles*: values that guide your actions so that you can live a full and meaningful life. However, even principles can bend somewhat to honor another principle. For example, it's important to tell the truth unless the truth hurts people needlessly. People tell little white lies from time to time, because to tell the truth at all times and in all circumstances can get in the way of having loving and caring relationships. When you single-mindedly follow a principle without regard to the situation in which you apply it, you serve a tyrant. Tyrants have little regard for the wishes and circumstances of others. Tyrants insist that you just follow their rules.

"Shoulds" are rules that pressure you and others to always act in a certain way, no matter what. "Shoulds" back you into a corner. They stress you out. "Shoulds" can make you anxious. When you believe that you *should always be on time* or that you *should never make mistakes*, your anxious mind makes things worse. "Shoulds" are the ultimate pattern of inflexible thinking. Furthermore, since "shoulds" are absolute rules—rules that apply to everyone, including you, at all times—when you break the rule, you might see yourself as bad or wrong. When you break "shoulds," you might feel intensely ashamed and guilty about things that other people are able to shrug off. When others don't live up to your "shoulds," you might feel needlessly angry and resentful. Roman believes he should always look cool and calm. He believes that he should always be the best and that being the best means always looking as if he is in complete control. Roman believes he should never look anxious or stressed, even when he's feeling anxious or stressed for good reasons. These "shoulds" only add to Roman's anxiety when he's in a situation in which other people likely would feel anxious too, such as when giving a presentation to several hundred attorneys.

Identifying Your Thinking Traps

To learn how to step outside your anxiety box, it's important that you know when you're in it and which thinking traps have boxed you in. Each time you feel anxious, write your anxious thoughts (what was going through your mind) and describe the situation you were in when this happened (see exercise 5.2). At times, you may wish to use the downward arrow technique (see above) to identify the anxious *hot thought* and then write that in the Anxious Thoughts column. Then, circle the type of thinking pattern that trapped you in the anxiety box. At times, one or more thinking traps might contribute to your anxious response. If that's the case, circle all that apply.

Exercise 5.2 Identify Your Thinking Traps Worksheet

Date/Time	Situation	Anxious Thoughts	Thinking Trap
			• Jumping to conclusions • Overfocusing • Thinking the worst • "Shoulds"
			• Jumping to conclusions • Overfocusing • Thinking the worst • "Shoulds"
			• Jumping to conclusions • Overfocusing • Thinking the worst • "Shoulds"
			• Jumping to conclusions • Overfocusing • Thinking the worst • "Shoulds"

THINKING OUTSIDE THE ANXIETY BOX

As you've learned, the problem isn't your anxious thoughts, but that you can't easily and quickly shift or change your anxious thoughts when you wish. Thinking traps maintain your anxious response, because they lock you into a pattern of interpreting things in a certain way. Thinking traps make it difficult for you to step outside the anxiety box to evaluate your situation more accurately, to raise your head to look around and decide whether or not you truly are in danger. However, with practice you can learn to step outside the anxiety box and slowly loosen your patterns of anxious thinking so that you can shift them when you wish.

In this section, you'll learn strategies for stepping outside the anxiety box. The strategies target the thinking traps common to most people with excessive anxiety or an anxiety disorder.

Reset Your "Predictometer"

In a sense, when you jump to conclusions, you tend to predict events in a certain way. We all do this and, thus, we all have a "predictometer": a thinking pattern that tends to interpret events in certain ways. As you've learned, the problem isn't that you have a predictometer, but that it often doesn't predict accurately. In other words, when you have excessive anxiety or an anxiety disorder, you have a predictometer that's a little out of whack. The two exercises that follow will reset your predictometer to help you predict events more accurately.

TESTING THE ACCURACY OF YOUR PREDICTIONS

An easy way to reset your predictometer is to test the accuracy of the predictions you make when you're feeling anxious and worried. Because your pattern of anxious thinking has you trapped into seeing things in a particular way, you might not often stop to ask yourself two important questions: *What prediction am I making?* and *How likely is it that this prediction is accurate?*

Using the worksheet in exercise 5.3, you'll track not only your predictions, but also their accuracy. Sometimes, realizing just how out of whack your predictometer is can help you shift your tendency to overfocus on scary outcomes. At times, this awareness alone is enough to help you step out of the anxiety box, at least for a moment.

Look at one of Tyra's Predictions Worksheets (sample exercise 5.3). Using several worksheets over two months, she wrote all her worst-case predictions about finding a job, her health, the welfare of her family, and the state of the world. At the end of two months, Tyra had quite a list. Of the thirty-seven anxious predictions that she had made, only one had come true (her mother had caught Tyra's cold). As the number of check marks increased every week, Tyra saw how often she overpredicted the likelihood that something bad would happen. Learning this helped her take her worries less seriously and to step out of the anxiety box for a bit whenever she found herself worrying too much and for too long.

Sample Exercise 5.3 Tyra's Predictions Worksheet

What terrible thing will happen and when?	Strength of Your Belief (0–100%)	What really happened?	Check False Predictions (√)
At my appointment tomorrow, the doctor will tell me that the mole on my face is cancerous.	85%	The doctor told me that the mole was not cancerous.	√
Someone is breaking into my car.	100%	The car alarm sounded because a big truck drove by and set it off.	√
My mother will catch my cold, get really sick, and not recover.	90%	My mother did catch my cold and was pretty sick, but she recovered quickly.	
My boss is going to fire me, because I was ten minutes late to take care of her kids so that she and her husband could go out to dinner.	80%	She asked me to try not to be late again, smiled at me, and went out to dinner. She didn't fire me.	√
My boss will fire me because her kids were awake when she and her husband returned from dinner.	70%	I explained that I had put them to bed and had stayed with them but that they hadn't been able to fall asleep. My boss was fine with this, and she understood. She didn't fire me.	√
My mother called, and I knew she was going to tell me that my sister had been in a car accident or that something else bad had happened to her.	70%	She chatted with me and told me that my sister and the rest of my family were fine.	√
I won't be able to do my job, because I'm so tired.	80%	I was tired, but the kids and my boss didn't seem to notice.	√

Every time you begin to worry intensely about something or imagine an outcome that makes you feel very anxious, record on the Predictions Worksheet (see exercise 5.3) exactly what bad thing you're predicting will happen and when. Then, indicate how strongly you believe the prediction (on a scale from 0 to 100 percent, where 100 percent means that you believe your prediction completely). Later fill in what really happened. If your prediction was false, place a check mark by it.

Exercise 5.3 Predictions Worksheet

What terrible thing will happen and when?	Strength of Your Belief (0–100%)	What really happened?	Check False Predictions (√)

Exercise 5.4 Calculate Your Validity Quotient

Through using your Predictions Worksheet for several weeks, you'll learn something about your day-to-day tendency to jump to scary conclusions. But you haven't been thinking this way for just a few weeks or a few months. You've likely been thinking this way for years. Jumping to scary conclusions every day is second nature to you, as you know by now, so it's not easy to step outside the anxiety box whenever you wish. To see your true tendency to jump to scary conclusions, it can help to calculate your Validity Quotient (Moses and Barlow 2006). To calculate your Validity Quotient, think back over the last five years (or one or two years), estimate the total number of times you predicted a particular scary conclusion (for example, *My boss will fire me tomorrow* or *This physical symptom means I have a terrible illness*), and estimate the total number of times this scary conclusion came true. Now, divide the number of scary predictions that came true by the total number of scary predictions. You can also calculate your Validity Quotient for all the scary predictions you made about all kinds of things in the past year. So, what do you think?

Prediction: _____

Q1:   How many times have you made this prediction during the past five years?   _____

Q2:   How many times during the past five years has the prediction come true?   _____

        Validity Quotient (Q2/Q1) x 100 percent   _____

Tyra calculated her Validity Quotient for her prediction that her boss would fire her from her job as a nanny. Tyra estimated that at least three times a month, she worried that her boss would fire her for one thing or another: three times per month, twelve months per year, for five years—that's 180 scary predictions. Tyra had had several bosses over the past five years, but a boss had never fired her and she had always received very positive recommendations. Her Validity Quotient was 0/100, or 0 percent. Tyra's Validity Quotient caught her attention. She'd never stopped to consider the accuracy of her predictions. Each prediction had seemed very true to her at the time. Tyra used her Validity Quotient to reset her predictometer when she was feeling anxious. She calculated her Validity Quotient for other worries too, such as scary predictions about her health or the safety of her family.

Step Back for a Second Look

Your anxious mind tends to jump to scary conclusions and then lock on them, making it difficult for you to step outside the anxiety box to look around to see whether or not you're really in danger. This is particularly true when the situation or event is ambiguous and could, therefore, be interpreted in several ways. If you have social anxiety or become very anxious in social situations, you'll understand what happens when you interpret a look on someone's face to mean that she's unhappy with you or that she thinks you're weird, boring, or annoying. Perhaps she does or doesn't think this. How do you know for sure? However, once your anxious mind latches on to a scary interpretation, it's tough to convince your anxious mind to let go of it.

You can learn, however, to loosen your anxious mind's grip on a scary interpretation by teaching it to step back for a second look. You likely can view any situation from other perspectives if you try. For example, in a large theater, there are many perspectives from which to view the stage—mezzanine, dress circle, grand tier—and every perspective is a bit different; for that reason, you pay a bit more or less for certain seats. Imagine that you're in the theater of your anxious interpretations and that you're moving from section to section in the balcony to take different looks at your anxious interpretation on the stage below you.

For example, Rosey used the View from the Balcony Worksheet (see sample exercise 5.5) to examine her interpretation that her principal thinks she's weird when he sees her blushing. She rated the probability (from 0 to 100 percent) that the interpretation that her principal thinks she's weird when he sees her blushing is correct. Then she brainstormed other possible views or explanations for the situation, and rated the likelihood of each. Then, she rerated the probability of her anxious interpretation.

Sample Exercise 5.5 Rosey's View from the Balcony Worksheet

Describe the event or situation:	*Speaking to my principal in the hallway and feeling as if I'm blushing.*	
Describe your anxious view (anxious interpretation):	*He thinks I'm weird because I'm blushing.*	**Probability Before (0–100%)**
		95%
		Probability After (0–100%)
		35%
Alternative, or other, views (from the balcony):		**Probability (0–100%)**
He thinks my face is red because I have a fever and am not feeling well.		85%
He thinks my face is red because I'm warm.		85%
He thinks my face is red because I'm tired.		75%
He thinks my face is red because I'm wearing makeup.		65%
He thinks my face is red because I've been running or moving at a fast pace.		75%

Now, you try it. Use the View from the Balcony Worksheet (exercise 5.5) to loosen your anxious mind's grip on a particular anxious interpretation. On the worksheet, write the event or situation briefly, along with your anxious interpretation. Rate the probability (from 0 to 100 percent) that your anxious interpretation is correct. Then brainstorm to find five to ten other possible views or explanations for the event or situation, and rate the likelihood that each alternative explanation is correct. Now, rerate the probability of your anxious interpretation. Does your probability estimation decrease as you step back to take a second look from the balcony?

With practice, you'll discover that your anxious mind is becoming more flexible and that you think of alternative explanations more quickly and easily. As your anxious mind becomes more flexible, you'll become less anxious and worried too.

Exercise 5.5 View from the Balcony Worksheet

Describe the event or situation:	*Speaking to my principal in the hallway and feeling as if I'm blushing.*	
Describe your anxious view (anxious interpretation):		**Probability Before** (0–100%)
		Probability After (0–100%)
Alternative, or other, views (from the balcony):		**Probability** (0–100%)

Jump Back from the Worst

One of the fastest ways to jump back from the worst-case scenario (to *de-catastrophize*) is to convince yourself that you could handle it if the worst possible outcome happened. To build your confidence in your ability to cope, it helps if you examine how you coped in the past. Then you can develop a plan for how to cope with the worst-case scenario (if it happens) in the future.

BUILD YOUR CONFIDENCE BY EXAMINING HOW YOU COPED IN THE PAST

Most people have faced difficult times and coped successfully. Coping successfully, however, doesn't mean that you get through a difficult situation without feeling intensely anxious, sad, frustrated, or hurt. Coping successfully means that you get through a difficult situation as best you can and feeling whatever you feel. Some people expect themselves to cope with a difficult situation without feeling difficult emotions, and furthermore, they believe that if they're feeling anxious, for example, they must not be coping with the difficult situation or must not be coping well. This couldn't be farther from the truth. Coping is about getting through each day until the days get easier. You've likely done this already, and thinking back over the ways in which you've handled difficult situations can increase your confidence that you'll handle the worst-case scenario again, if it happens.

Use the "How I Coped in the Past" Worksheet (see exercise 5.6) to examine the ways in which you've handled difficult situations in the past. List five times or situations in the past that were difficult for you. For each crisis, write the specific ways in which you coped. Write the names of friends you called. Jot down the strategies you used to manage your anxiety or sadness—for example, exercise, medications, mindfulness, or hobbies. Note the personal resources you used to get through the day—for example, your research skills, your ability to negotiate with others, or your ability to understand complicated financial matters. Across these crises, which coping strategy helped the most? Did you rely on a particular coping strategy more often than not, and was it usually helpful? Did you try any strategy that you had never used before or haven't used often, and how did that work for you?

Tyra completed a "How I Coped in the Past" Worksheet for the time she lost her job working for an event planner. She had loved the job and been surprised when the company let her go after only ten months. Although she had known the company was in financial trouble, she took this very hard and blamed herself. Tyra noticed that an important way she had coped with this setback was to lean on her friends and family. She had been uncomfortable doing so, and it had been difficult to tell her friends and family that she had lost her job. However, she could see how helpful it had been for her to reach out to others. Realizing that she had a strong and caring support system made the possibility of losing her current job a little less scary.

Sample Exercise 5.6 Tyra's "How I Coped in the Past" Worksheet

Difficult Situation in the Past	Ways I Coped with That Situation
I lost a job I loved, working for an event planner.	I called my mother and sister, who visited me for a few days to help me get my mind off it.
	I asked my then boss to write a letter of recommendation, and it was a great letter that helped me feel much better.
	I called my best friend, who helped me update my résumé and went with me to look for a new job.
	I started free yoga classes at the YWCA, which helped with my stress.
	I called some of my coworkers at the event-planning company, and they reminded me that I had lost my job because the company was downsizing and I was the most recent hire.

Exercise 5.6 "How I Coped in the Past" Worksheet

Difficult Situation in the Past	Ways I Coped with That Situation

CREATE A PLAN TO JUMP BACK FROM THE WORST

If you have a plan to jump back from the worst, you'll feel less anxious about the worst-case scenario, because you'll know how to cope with it if it happens. Imagine that you're facing the worst: a serious illness, the loss of your job, the end of a relationship, whatever catastrophe you fear. As difficult as this imagined scenario might be, you're not going to roll over and surrender, even if that's what you believe you would do. You'll try to cope with it—for yourself and for those who care about you.

Tyra created a Plan to Jump Back from the Worst for her chronic worry that her boyfriend would break up with her and that she would be unable to handle the loss and her feelings of loneliness. Pete, her boyfriend, showed no signs that he was unhappy with Tyra or their relationship, but this didn't stop thoughts from running through Tyra's mind every day about when and how Pete would tell her that he's had enough. In fact, Tyra realized that the only thing that rocked her relationship with Pete somewhat was that she couldn't stop worrying about a breakup.

Sample Exercise 5.7 Tyra's Plan to Jump Back from the Worst

Describe your worst-case prediction:	*My boyfriend leaves me because I'm such a mess.*	Ability to Cope Before (0–100%)
		20%
What are my strengths and resources that will help me cope?	*I've experienced losses before and survived. I'm smart and I can think on my feet. I have a caring and supportive family and network of friends. I meet people easily, and people like me and think I'm fun. I'm not broke, and I work hard. I've put away a nice nest egg, and I could use that if I had to.*	
What can I do to help myself cope?	*I could use my savings to take a little vacation and hang out with friends. I could use some of the tools I've learned to calm my body and mind. I like the View from the Balcony Worksheet, and that will help. I like some of the other tools in the book too. They'll help me stay centered and calm. Maybe I'll join a club or do some of the things I never did because Pete wasn't interested. That will help keep my mind off missing him.*	
What can I say to myself (or remind myself of) to help myself cope?	*I'm a survivor. I've been through breakups before and they were painful, but I always got through them. I have friends and family who love me. Pete is a good guy, and even if we break up, I know he'll do it in a decent way. We might even stay friends.*	
Whom can I speak to or seek support from to help me cope?	*I'll call my mother and sister. They're good listeners. Maybe I'll visit them for a week or two. I'll get together with my close friends. They love and care about me.*	
What are other ways to cope?	*Find ways to be around people: hang out in coffee shops, visit parks, and do other fun things.*	Ability to Cope After (0–100%)
		80%

On the worksheet, write a brief description of your worst-case prediction and rate how confident you feel (0 to 100 percent) that you could handle or cope with the worst if it happened. Now, brainstorm ten or twelve ways in which you might cope with the worst. For ideas about ways to cope, consider your strengths. Are you a good problem solver? Do you get along with people? Do you have some savings to get you through tough times? Are you resourceful and good at thinking on your feet? What are the things you could do to cope?

Exercise 5.7 Plan to Jump Back from the Worst

		Ability to Cope Before (0–100%)
Describe your worst-case prediction:		
What are my strengths and resources that will help me cope?		
What can I do to help myself cope?		
What can I say to myself (or remind myself of) to help myself cope?		
Whom can I speak to or seek support from to help me cope?		
What are other ways to cope?		**Ability to Cope After (0–100%)**

Recall how you coped with hard times in the past. What did you do to get through the day? What tools have you learned in this book to calm your anxious mind and body? What can you say to yourself that would help you cope? Do you have affirmations or inspirational quotes that help? What are the things that friends say to you that help, and can you say those things to yourself?

Consider your sources of emotional and social support. Which of your family members and friends are good listeners who have helped you through tough times? Do you have a therapist or physician who's there for you? Perhaps you have a coworker who's good at something that would help you solve a problem that's making life hard for you. Now, rerate how confident you feel (0 to 100 percent) that you could handle or cope with the worst if it happened. Now that you've created your Plan to Jump Back from the Worst, have your feelings about your worst-case prediction changed? Do you feel a little less worried about the "catastrophe" if it were to happen? Do you feel less overwhelmed and afraid?

Break Free from the Tyranny of "Shoulds"

For many anxious people, "shoulds" are second nature, so it's not easy to break free from the tyranny that holds their anxious mind hostage. However, you can break free from, or at least soften, the "shoulds" and rules that keep you trapped in the anxiety box.

Exercise 5.8 Count the "Shoulds"

An easy way to break free from the tyranny of "shoulds" is to count them. Most people are unaware of the number of times they think or say the word "should," or the number of "shoulds" that appear in sheep's clothing: the "musts," "have tos," "got tos," and "ought tos." For a week or two, use a golf-stroke counter or another simple counter to count the number of times you think or say the word "should" (or its other forms). If you don't have a counter, place pennies in one pocket and transfer a penny to the other pocket each time you think or say "should," and then place the "should" pennies (or other tokens if you're short of pennies) in a jar so that you can see the full weight of the tyranny under which you live. As you become more aware of how often your "shoulds" push you around, you'll find it easier to let go of "shoulds" and watch them drift away.

BALANCE THE "SHOULD"

You might often ask yourself, *Why don't I do the things I should?* For example, you might skip exercise for a week, despite knowing that exercise lessens your stress and makes you feel better in a hundred ways. You might take a second helping of potatoes, although you know that the first helping was enough. You might avoid seeing friends, despite knowing that when you do spend time with them, you enjoy yourself and are glad you did it. Why you do some things and don't do other things is complicated. Many factors can lessen your will to do something on one day versus another.

In other words, you avoid doing what you believe you should do because on a particular day, the costs of doing it outweigh the benefits. The costs might include your anxiety: today you feel more anxious going to the store than you did last week. You might put off doing something because you don't understand how to do it and want to learn more about how to do it before trying it. You might put off doing what you did last week, because it's more inconvenient to do today than next week. Regardless of the costs or the benefits of doing or not doing something, however, a "should" doesn't really tip the scale in a way that prompts you to always do what you wish to do. In fact, how many times have you told yourself you should do something, and then didn't do it? "Shoulds" don't really work, and they make life much harder, to boot.

If you understand your reasons for wishing to do or not do something—rather than relying on a "should" to push you to try it—you might feel less anxious, guilty, and frustrated. Using the Balance the "Should" Worksheet (exercise 5.9), describe the situation and the rule, or "should," that's making you anxious (or guilty or frustrated). Then, list the costs of following the rule in the Costs column and the benefits of following the rule in the Benefits column. Do the same cost-benefit comparison for *not* following the rule. Learning to examine the costs and benefits, rather than relying on the "should," to guide your decisions is the key to developing more flexible decision making.

Rosey completed a Balance the "Should" Worksheet when she noticed she was telling herself, *I shouldn't blush*, during meetings with her principal. She could see that she suffered many costs to thinking this way and little real upside. This helped her accept that perhaps stating her wish as a preference (*I would prefer not to blush in my meetings with my principal*) rather than a "should" could make future meetings a little less stressful for her.

Sample Exercise 5.9 Balance the "Should" Worksheet

Situation:	Meeting with my principal to discuss the upcoming school-holiday festival.	
Rule ("should") that was broken:	I shouldn't blush when I speak with him.	
	Following the Rule ("Should")	
	Costs	**Benefits**
	I'll feel more anxious. I'll feel bad about myself if I do blush. Trying to control something I can't control will only make me feel worse about myself. I won't be able to focus as well on what my principal is saying, which will make me worry more about missing something.	If I could prevent myself from blushing, I would feel less worried, but it's impossible to not blush when I'm anxious.
	***Not* Following the Rule ("Should")**	
	Costs	**Benefits**
	My principal may see that I'm blushing and think I'm weird, but I'm learning that this is how my anxious mind thinks and is not necessarily the way things are.	I'll feel less anxious about trying to stop something I can't control. I'll be able to focus more on what he's saying. I may see that blushing or not blushing makes no difference in what happens. I'll feel less upset with myself if I do blush, because I won't be breaking a "should" too.

Exercise 5.9 Balance the "Should" Worksheet

Situation:	
Rule ("should") that was broken:	

	Following the Rule ("Should")	
	Costs	**Benefits**

	***Not* Following the Rule ("Should")**	
	Costs	**Benefits**

You can use this same strategy when you're frustrated or angry with other people because they didn't do what you thought they should do. If you try it, consider the costs and benefits to the person of following or breaking the "should," or rule. You might discover that that person has good reasons (even if you don't agree with those reasons) for doing what he wants to do.

Taking It Out on Your Anxious Mind

Once you become aware of your tendency to interpret things in particular ways—your thinking traps—you might blame your anxious mind for working this way. You might think, *I can't believe I fell into that thinking trap again. I'm such an idiot.* This only makes things worse. The more you blame yourself for the way your anxious mind works, the more you'll try to control or reject your anxious thoughts, and the more rigid your thinking pattern then becomes. It's important that you learn to observe your anxious thoughts without judging them, and the mindfulness strategies you learned in chapter 4 ("Watching and Waiting") will help you do that. Other strategies can help too, such as defusion.

DEFUSION

You might have noticed that sometimes, no matter how hard you try, you can't reason your way out of the anxiety box, nor can you ignore what your anxious mind tells you. As you become more and more anxious, you and your thoughts become one: you no longer *have* anxious thoughts; you *are* your anxious thoughts. In other words, you have "fused" tightly with your anxious thoughts, and now these thoughts seem far more important and more real than perhaps they really are. Once you are fused with your anxious thoughts, you're headed for more anxiety and suffering. However, you can learn to unhook from your anxious thoughts and take a time-out from believing what your anxious mind tells you. You can learn to defuse your anxious thoughts in order to step outside the anxiety box.

Defusion strategies (Hayes 2005; Hayes, Strosahl, and Wilson 1999) help you detach from your anxious thoughts, thereby allowing you to take them less seriously. An easy exercise to help you understand how defusion works is a language game (Hayes 2005; Titchener 1910).

Exercise 5.10 MilkMilkMilk

Find a quiet and private place where you can speak without being overheard. First, try the following visualization.

Close your eyes and imagine that you're opening a container of fresh, cold milk. Feel the container in your hand. Notice the cool dampness of the jar and its weight and texture. Imagine pouring the milk from the container into a glass. Hear the sound of the milk as it flows into the glass. Smell the milk and take a sip. Rest your mind on this image now. Perhaps at this moment, you can taste the faint flavor of milk in your mouth, even though you aren't drinking milk.

Our minds have this amazing ability to code sensory experiences, such as taste and texture, into symbols like the word "milk." Now, moments before we drink milk, our minds prepare for a particular sensory experience. That's why we're often surprised when we expect one taste, such as cool, fresh milk, and get another: the taste of warm, soured milk. It also works the other way. We invite into our minds the word "milk," and we experience the sensory impressions associated with this word. Our minds can transform symbols like the word "milk" into imaginary sense impressions.

Since the word "milk" is just a symbol for the sensory experience of "milk," you can play around with the symbol a bit to change the experience. Say the word "milk" aloud over and over as fast as you can, while still pronouncing it clearly. Say the word "milk" in this way for about forty-five seconds. What did you notice?

Most people notice that the meaning of the word "milk" fades after they have repeated it for a while. The word "milk" becomes a nonsense sound that no longer brings forth vivid sensory impressions of the white, wet, and cool liquid you know as milk. Did you notice that the word "milk" began to sound odd, like any other odd sound: *baabaabaa* or *saasaasaa*? This rarely happens in a conversation, when the sounds are words with particular meanings. It's difficult to hear just the sounds when we're speaking with someone, because the meanings, rather than the sounds, grab our attention. The same is true for thoughts.

Thoughts bring forth particular meanings that evoke certain emotions. This is the anxious mind at work. Defusion strategies will help you shift the meaning of the thoughts that make you anxious so that you can more easily detach from them, rendering them less likely to intensify your anxious response. There are many great defusion strategies. If the following strategies help, check out *Mind and Emotions: A Universal Treatment for Emotional Disorders* (New Harbinger Publications, 2011) and *Get Out of Your Mind and Into Your Life: The New Acceptance and Commitment Therapy* (New Harbinger Publications, 2005) for additional strategies.

Exercise 5.11 Label an Anxious Thought

You can defuse from an anxious thought by labeling it: describing the thought as something your mind produces, rather than something you are or do. This distinction between a thought and an action, or a characteristic about you or the situation you're in, is at the heart of defusion. When you have a distressing thought, feeling, or urge, try labeling it in one of the following ways.

Look at how Tyra (who has generalized anxiety disorder) labeled her anxious thoughts:

I'm having the thought that *I'll never find a full-time job*   .

I'm having the feeling that   .

I'm having a memory or image of *being a nanny forever*   .

I'm having the body sensation that   .

I'm having a desire to *stop looking for a new job*   .

Now when Tyra begins to worry that she might never find a full-time job, she says to herself, *I'm having the thought that I'll never find a full-time job*, which helps her unhook from the worry.

Now you try it:

I'm having the thought that   .
(describe your thought)

I'm having the feeling that   .
(describe your emotion)

I'm having a memory or image of   .
(describe your memory or image)

I'm having the body sensation that   .
(describe your body sensation)

I'm having a desire to   .
(describe your urge to do something)

Exercise 5.12 Take the Long Way around an Anxious Thought

You can defuse an anxious thought by "taking the long way around it." Taking the long way around an anxious thought is when you describe the thought, sensation, or urge with a longer, wordier description. For example, you can defuse the short, scary anxious thought *What if I lose my job* by taking the long way around it: *My mind is once again having that very familiar and "oh, so scary" thought—a thought that enters my mind over and over again without variation and without merit—that I might lose my job.* Taking the long way around an anxious thought creates some distance between you and that thought so that you can examine it with clearer eyes.

When the Problem Is What the Thought Means

Your anxious mind gets your attention. Your mind grips you and pulls you inside the anxiety box, where your anxious thoughts seem more important than they really are. This is particularly true when you place a meaning on a thought: this thought means I'm in danger, or that thought means I'm a bad person. With meanings like these, you'll want to push the thoughts from your mind, but our anxious minds don't work that way. The harder we try to push a thought out of the anxiety box, the harder it pushes its way back inside (Wegner 1994).

It's quite common to have strange thoughts that don't make sense. Most people easily let go of these thoughts by telling themselves, *That's a silly thought*, and soon their minds are on to other things. Some people, particularly people with obsessive-compulsive disorder, however, can't easily let go of certain thoughts, particularly when the thoughts enter their anxious minds with great power and force. Thoughts that enter our awareness with this kind of power are intrusive. Some people can have intrusive thoughts that they might hurt a loved one or molest a child. They might have intrusive thoughts that go against their moral or religious beliefs and values, such as unwanted sexual thoughts or images of Satan.

Thoughts such as these are automatic—in the same way that anxious thoughts are automatic—but there's an important difference. Intrusive thoughts don't make much sense, so it's not easy or helpful to reason with them. For example, you can't reason with a thought that predicts that if you touch your kitchen counter and don't wash your hands afterward, you'll die—because the likelihood of that happening is already near zero. Or, if you challenge the thought *I'm a child molester* with the question *What's the worst that can happen, and how bad is that?* you're not likely to come back with an answer that helps you feel less anxious.

Instead, a more effective strategy is to learn to unhook from the *meaning* of an intrusive, nonsensical thought by changing what you think it might mean to *have* that intrusive thought.

UNHOOK FROM THE MEANING TO UNHOOK FROM THE THOUGHT

To unhook from the thought, you'll want to unhook from its meaning first. Use the downward arrow technique (review exercise 5.1) you learned earlier to identify the hot intrusive thought, but this time, ask yourself different questions about the thought: *How does having this thought make me feel? What do I think having this thought means about me? What do I think having this thought means might happen?*

Look how Bart identified his hot intrusive thought (sample exercise 5.13). Notice that the hot thought was what he believed it meant to have the intrusive thought *I have germs on my hands.* In other words, he thought that having the thought was enough to kill him. That's why intrusive thoughts don't make sense.

Sample Exercise 5.13 Bart's Identify Your Hot Intrusive Thought Worksheet

Automatic appraisal: *I have germs on my hands.*

What do I think having this thought means might happen?
What do I think having this thought means I might do?
What do I think having this thought means about me?
How does having this thought make me feel?

Underlying appraisal: *This thought means I'm more likely to get sick.*

What do I think having this thought means might happen?
What do I think having this thought means I might do?
What do I think having this thought means about me?
How does having this thought make me feel?

Underlying appraisal: *This thought means I'm more likely to die from some disease.*

Exercise 5.13 Identify Your Hot Intrusive Thought Worksheet

Automatic appraisal: _____

What do I think having this thought means might happen?
What do I think having this thought means I might do?
What do I think having this thought means about me?
How does having this thought make me feel?

Underlying appraisal: _____

What do I think having this thought means might happen?
What do I think having this thought means I might do?
What do I think having this thought means about me?
How does having this thought make me feel?

Underlying appraisal: _____

What do I think having this thought means might happen?
What do I think having this thought means I might do?
What do I think having this thought means about me?
How does having this thought make me feel?

Underlying appraisal: _____

What do I think having this thought means might happen?
What do I think having this thought means I might do?
What do I think having this thought means about me?
How does having this thought make me feel?

The thoughts about, or meanings placed on, an intrusive and nonsensical thought turn it into an anxious thought. One person might have a horrible intrusive thought that he can easily shake off, because he interprets that thought as just an intrusive, silly thought and reasons that it doesn't mean anything about him or what he might do. Another person might have the same intrusive thought but interpret it to mean something horrible about him or that he will act on the thought and do something he doesn't want to do.

Next, use the strategies you've learned to think outside the anxiety box to generate different interpretations about having an intrusive thought.

Jumping to conclusions. *What's the likelihood that having the thought* I have germs on my hands *means I'm more likely to get sick and die?* Bart looked for alternative explanations to what it meant to have this thought: *I had thoughts like this before, and nothing bad happened. I've even had this thought and couldn't wash my hands, and I didn't die. Thoughts don't increase the likelihood that I'll get sick. Thoughts aren't germs.*

Overfocusing on the conclusions. Bart used strategies to shift his overfocus on the meaning of the thoughts: *Just because I'm having the thought* I have germs on my hands *many times a day doesn't make the thought important. If I step back and look at this thought—as if from the balcony—I realize that this thought isn't any more important than any other thought I have every day. Just because I have this thought many times each day doesn't make it truer or increase the likelihood that something bad will happen. When I give the thought* I have germs on my hands *more importance than it deserves, then the thought grows bigger and scarier in my anxious mind.*

Last, you can defuse the intrusive thought to reduce the importance you attach to it. Through defusion, you can learn to view an intrusive thought as just another thought, not one that's meaningful, important, or significant in some way. You can apply the MilkMilkMilk exercise (earlier in this chapter) to your intrusive thought *The counter is covered in germs, and I might die at any moment* by repeating the thought aloud over and over. You can sing the intrusive thought to your favorite melody over and over, or repeat the intrusive thought over and over in a baby voice or that of your favorite cartoon character. You can repeat the intrusive thought backward or repeat every other word: *Counter covered germs I die any.* You can defuse the importance of the intrusive thought to loosen its grip on you.

Learning ways to step outside the anxiety box will help you feel less anxious, because looking at your anxious response from outside-in can help you see that the magnitude of your anxious response doesn't make sense, given the situation. However, learning to step outside your anxiety box will not necessarily help you live a fuller and freer life. To live a fuller and freer life, it's important to also break free from the pattern of avoidance that has constricted your life and made each day a little harder to live.

In the next chapter, you'll learn strategies to break free from the pattern of avoidance—another pattern that has boxed you in. Learning to step toward discomfort—also known as "exposure"—is the most important part of any plan to recover from excessive anxiety or an anxiety disorder. All that you've learned so far will prepare you for, and increase your willingness to try, these next important steps. As you practice stepping toward discomfort, you'll spend more and more time outside your anxiety box, which is how true, deep, and corrective change occurs. The more time you spend outside your anxiety box looking in, the more deeply you'll believe that you have nothing to fear.

CHAPTER 6

Stepping toward Discomfort

All the skills you've learned thus far are for a single purpose: to decrease your fear enough to instill *willingness* to try this final and most important skill—stepping toward discomfort. Stepping toward discomfort, also referred to as "exposure," is the way to real and deep change—in what you believe about the things that make you anxious and, just as important, in what you believe about your anxious response itself. Change like this only happens when you face your fear: when you confront the object or situation that frightens you.

In this chapter, you'll learn a systematic way to step toward discomfort and soon experience the benefits of turning your anxious response on its head. First, the chapter describes the advantages of stepping toward discomfort, followed by what stepping toward discomfort practice is and is not. Later, you'll learn how to build a stepping-toward-discomfort ladder and the strategies you can use to approach anxiety-provoking situations, images, and physical sensations.

ADVANTAGES OF STEPPING TOWARD DISCOMFORT

Stepping toward discomfort is about changing an old habit you've likely developed over many years: avoiding or stepping away from what makes you uncomfortable or anxious. This part of your anxious response is likely the most debilitating, because avoidance—more than the uncomfortable feelings themselves—truly interferes with your wish to live a full and meaningful life.

Learning to step toward (rather than away from) what makes you anxious or uncomfortable is the formula for breaking the old habit of avoiding or neutralizing your anxious response. It might take two to six weeks to build this new habit or pattern, but in time, this new habit will be second nature to you. You'll automatically step into discomfort. Without thinking much about it, you'll resist the urge to neutralize your anxious response, by washing your hands or checking locks repeatedly, for example, to look away, or to step away from the objects and situations that frighten you. As you build this new habit, your life will open again, because you'll free yourself from the avoidance that has held you back from living your life fully.

Learning to step toward discomfort isn't easy. In fact, you might think stepping toward discomfort is the hardest part of recovering from your anxiety disorder—and you'd be correct. However, as you become more comfortable stepping toward discomfort, you'll realize that as difficult as it is, it's the key to real and deep change. Stepping toward discomfort is the path along which you'll learn the truth about your anxious response, about yourself, and about the world in which you live.

First, you'll learn that your anxious response is not dangerous. Your anxious response is neither permanent nor fatal, and it peaks but always goes away, whether you do anything to lessen it or not. When you learn this, you'll fear your anxious response less. Second, you'll learn that stepping toward discomfort gives you *more* of a sense of mastery over your anxious response, not less. Because you make the conscious decision to step toward (rather than away from) your discomfort, you'll feel less pressured and thereby less anxious. Third, as you step toward discomfort, you'll learn that you can handle the situation and your anxious response. Furthermore, you'll learn that what you fear or worry about never happens or rarely happens. Fourth, you'll learn that your old pattern of avoiding what makes you uncomfortable can change, and as it changes, breaking the pattern as it arises in the future becomes easier. Fifth, through resisting your anxious actions, you'll learn that they don't really work the way you think they do. You'll learn that nothing bad happens if you don't use your anxious actions and, just as important, that you can handle your anxious response without any assistance—from other people or your anxious actions. This is learning at a deep level.

What Stepping toward Discomfort Is and Is Not

Stepping toward discomfort is learning to face, rather than turn away from, your anxious response. As you face your anxious response, you'll grow more confident and less anxious. You may be thinking, *I face my anxious response sometimes, and it doesn't work*. However, the principle of facing your anxious response isn't the problem. Researchers have demonstrated over many years that facing our fears now helps us feel less fearful in the future. The problem, then, hasn't been the principle of facing your anxious response, but the way you have gone about it. To benefit fully from every practice, it's essential that you practice each step on the stepping-toward-discomfort ladder (which you'll build later in the chapter) in a particular way. Stepping toward discomfort practice or exposure is:

Intentional. Always plan the practice. Stepping toward discomfort practice is never a surprise. Sometimes, you might have unexpectedly found yourself in a situation that made you anxious or uncomfortable. For example, you might have become afraid when you drove onto the freeway by accident after missing a turn; or you might have become anxious on realizing that you had to sit through a meeting, but not near the exit the way you usually do. This is not true practice. These are accidents that you get through and then hope won't happen to you again. Practice, on the other hand, is intentional and planned. You decide where to start on your stepping-toward-discomfort ladder and when.

Frequent. Effective practice in stepping toward discomfort means that you repeat the practice until you experience real change in the intensity and duration of your anxious response. At times, you might have decided to face your anxious response, only to discover that you became more anxious than you had anticipated, so you lost your nerve. Infrequent practice decreases confidence, because it's difficult to master something that frightens you if you practice just once or only a few times. For example, driving on the freeway once a month is much less effective than doing so several times a week to overcome your fear of driving. Effective practice, then, is repeated practice that continues until you have mastered a particular step on your practice ladder. Additionally, you'll recover from your anxiety problems or disorder faster and with less discomfort if you practice stepping toward discomfort thirty or forty minutes a day, rather than five minutes a day. The more you put into it, the faster you'll recover.

Sufficient. For your stepping toward discomfort practice to be effective in the long term, it's essential that you get the most out of every practice. You'll learn more about this later in the chapter, but typically, sufficient practice means continuing the practice until you experience a significant decrease in anxiety. For example, driving on the freeway *for as long as I can* might mean driving ten minutes one day and twenty minutes another day, depending on what you believe you can handle. This approach isn't any more helpful than setting a goal of practicing until you can no longer tolerate your anxious response. This only reinforces your tendency to escape when you believe that your anxiety is unbearable. Sufficient practice means remaining with your anxious response until you master it.

Fully. Effective practice means commiting fully to feeling your anxious response without giving in to urges to resist it. Distracting yourself when you practice stepping toward discomfort prevents you from learning what's important for you to learn. For example, if you distract yourself from your anxious response, you might believe you couldn't have handled it if you had remained fully with it. Similarly, anything you do—subtle or not so subtle—to lessen your anxious response detracts from the full benefit of the practice. Sitting in a seat at the end of a row in the theater, with an eye on the exit, is not a fully engaged practice. Touching something that's dirty and wiping your hands on a damp rag, rather than washing your hands, is a step in the right direction but not a full and effective practice. Furthermore, relying on friends or family to help you practice facing your fears might increase your willingness to practice, but will dilute the effectiveness of your recovery unless you practice the same things without friends or family. You'll learn more about getting the most out of every practice later in the chapter, when you learn to "FACE" your anxious response.

BUILDING YOUR STEPPING-TOWARD-DISCOMFORT SITUATIONAL PRACTICE LADDER

The first step in practicing stepping toward discomfort is to build a practice ladder. You'll start with a situational practice ladder, which lists specific objects or situations that trigger your anxious response, ranked in order of the intensity of that anxious response. For example, if you're afraid to drive on freeways, some stretches of freeway likely make you more anxious than others. Your situational practice ladder might then include the specific freeways (or sections of freeways) that make you anxious, ranked from the freeway section that makes you least anxious to the one that would make you the most anxious, if you were to drive it. The situational practice ladder, as well as other practice ladders you'll build later, is an essential part of your recovery. The ladder will make the practices a bit easier, and more important, you'll use it to decide where to start each practice. The practice ladder is the best way to ensure that your anxiety will be in a manageable range, which will increase your willingness to practice stepping toward discomfort. Use the ladder rather than anxious actions or avoidance strategies to lessen your anxiety when you practice. If you're too anxious to remain in a particular situation, step down the ladder to the next situation until you're anxious, but not so anxious that you can't remain in the situation. Furthermore, when you use the ladder to adjust your anxiety level, you'll find that you're better able to resist your anxious actions, because you're practicing in a range where your anxious response is neither too high nor too low. In this way, you'll get the full benefit from every practice and be more likely to try the next one.

Step 1: List situations that trigger your anxious response. To build your situational practice ladder, think about the situations that trigger your anxious response. Consider situations that you avoid or that trigger other anxious actions, such as checking, distracting yourself, and seeking reassurance about things that worry you. For example, Rosey, the teacher with social anxiety disorder, applies heavy makeup to decrease the likelihood that people will notice if she blushes. Rosey could include on her ladder two or three steps where she applies less and less makeup. A final, slightly over-the-top step might be for Rosey to apply makeup that makes her appear to *be* blushing.

The best situations are ones that you can initiate without assistance. For example, if you have social anxiety disorder, you might fear offering your opinion about this or that. Rather than waiting for someone to share an opinion so that you can share yours, ask people what they thought about the movie, the food, or the weather, and then give your opinion. In this way, you create more opportunities to practice. You might list, "Ask someone's opinion and then give mine." Also, make certain the situations are ones that you can repeat frequently within a week. For example, if you have claustrophobia (fear of enclosed spaces), you might avoid flying. Unless you have the time and money to fly several times per week, it will be difficult for you to fly enough times to master your anxious response. However, you might be able to wear a mask or sit in a small closet (which likely will trigger claustrophobic feelings similar to those you feel when you're flying) several times per week to master your anxious response.

Try to develop a list that covers the range of your anxious response: situations that trigger low, moderate, and high levels of anxiety or fear. For example, Roman, who has panic disorder and is afraid to drive on freeways and surface streets, listed "driving long and short distances on busy and quiet streets, and on certain stretches of freeways." Bart, who has obsessive-compulsive disorder, listed situations in his home and at school that triggered his anxious response. For example, his list included touching the kitchen counter, floor, windowsills, and toilet seat at home and at school. Try to describe each situation in as specific and detailed a way as possible. For example, rather than "looking down from a high place," describe the situation as "looking down from a balcony while standing three feet away from the railing." Look at Roman's initial list of situations for his practice ladder. He included items that he tended to avoid because they triggered his anxious response in the past, and situations where he remembered relying on other anxious actions (gripping handrails, looking away, seeking reassurance from his wife) to get him through the moment.

Roman's Initial List of Situations for His Practice Ladder

1. *Driving on surface streets in my neighborhood.*

2. *Driving the freeway from home to work.*

3. *Riding up the escalator.*

4. *Riding down the escalator.*

5. *Standing on a balcony looking down.*

6. *Standing on the subway platform, looking down at the tracks.*

7. *Standing six steps up a ladder.*

8. *Looking out the conference-room window on the twenty-fourth floor.*

9. *Standing in a stairwell and looking down the stairs.*

10. *Looking down from the second floor of the parking garage.*

You may wish to create practice ladders for different situations, when a situation is particularly difficult for you. For example, Roman later developed a separate ladder because escalators were particularly challenging for him. The escalator ladder included shorter escalators and longer escalators, and riding when escalators were crowded and less crowded.

Step 2: Adjust situations based on what influences your anxious response. Typically, there are certain variables that influence your anxious response. *Proximity* to an object or situation can influence the degree of your anxious response. For example, Roman knew that heights tended to trigger the dizzy feelings he feared. For Roman, proximity to a ledge or overlook influenced his anxious response. He was more anxious when standing five feet away from a balcony, for example, than ten feet away. The *time* you spend in a feared situation, experiencing a feared physical sensation, or near a feared object is another variable that can influence the intensity of your anxious response. Rosey, for example, feared that others would notice that she was blushing and then think she was weird or incompetent. Rosey then avoided eye contact with certain people, such as other teachers and, especially, her principal. Rosey felt more anxious about looking into her principal's face for five minutes while speaking with him than for two minutes. The final variable that can influence your anxious response is the *size* or *degree* of something. For example, if you're afraid of dogs, you might be more anxious around a large dog than a small one. For Bart, the intensity of his anxious response was influenced by the degree to which he perceived something was dirty or germ laden. Touching the toilet seat in his bathroom at home triggered more anxiety and more-intense urges to wash his hands than touching his kitchen counter.

Step 3: Rank situations from easiest to most difficult. Now, it's time to rank the situations on a 0-to-100 scale, based on how anxious you think you'd feel if you stepped toward discomfort right now, without taking any anxious actions to decrease your anxiety during the situation. On this scale:

0 = no fear or discomfort.

25 = some fear or discomfort.

50 = moderate fear or discomfort.

75 = strong fear or discomfort.

100 = extreme fear or discomfort.

Try to adjust the features of the situation so that no two situations trigger the same level of anxiety. To help with this, you can write the situations on slips of paper and lay them out on the floor in order of lowest to highest anxiety, taking care that each slip of paper is a rung on the ladder. If two situations feel as if they would be equally difficult, ask yourself which you would rather do first. You'll likely select the one that's a little easier, and you can place that one below the other one on your ladder. Here is Roman's practice ladder for his fear that he would faint and fall from a high place.

Sample Exercise 6.1a Roman's Situational Practice Ladder

In the "Situation" column, Roman listed a variety of situations, and then rated (using the 0-to-100 scale) in the "Anxiety" column how much anxiety he would feel if he were to practice each one now. Roman listed the situations in order of difficulty, with the most difficult situations (those arousing the most anxiety) near the top and the least difficult situations (those evoking the least anxiety) near the bottom.

0	25	50	75	100
No fear or discomfort	Some fear or discomfort	Moderate fear or discomfort	Strong fear or discomfort	Extreme fear or discomfort

Situation	Anxiety (0–100)
1. *Ride down the escalator.*	*100*
2. *Stand on the subway platform, three feet away from the edge, looking down at the tracks.*	*90*
3. *Stand on a balcony, one foot away from the railing, looking down.*	*80*
4. *Stand in a stairwell, one foot from the edge of the step, looking down the stairs.*	*70*
5. *Stand six steps up a ladder.*	*60*
6. *Look down from the second floor of the parking garage, one foot away from the railing.*	*50*
7. *Drive home from work on the freeway, on the section that dips down toward the valley.*	*40*
8. *Look out the conference-room window on the twenty-fourth floor, while standing one foot away from the window.*	*30*
9. *Drive on surface streets in my neighborhood.*	*20*
10. *Ride up the escalator.*	*10*

Step 4: Identify the anxious actions you'll resist, and do the opposite. To get the most out of every stepping-toward-discomfort practice, it's essential that you resist doing any anxious actions to lessen your anxious response. You'll learn more about this later in the chapter and in chapter 7 ("Keeping Going"), where you'll learn how "opposite action" can protect you from sliding back into your old pattern of avoidance (Linehan 1993; Allen, McHugh, and Barlow 2008; Moses and Barlow 2006). Of course, stepping toward discomfort is the opposite of avoidance, which is the habit you're trying to break. However, it can help to think about how you could do the opposite of other anxious actions. For example, when Roman stands on the subway platform, he avoids looking down at the tracks and stays away from the edge. He even leans back a little, just in case he feels dizzy. Furthermore, he likes to stay away from other people, because he fears that if he's dizzy or light-headed, people might accidentally push him toward the edge of the platform. Roman took these anxious actions and turned them on their heads so that he could practice stepping toward discomfort without any of his typical anxious actions.

Sample Exercise 6.1b Roman's Situational Practice Ladder with Do the Opposite

In the "Do the Opposite Action" column, Roman listed next to each situation his opposite action (as opposed to anxious action) so that he would know to resist doing the anxious action when he practiced stepping toward discomfort.

Practice Ladder with Do the Opposite

0	25	50	75	100
No fear or discomfort	Some fear or discomfort	Moderate fear or discomfort	Strong fear or discomfort	Extreme fear or discomfort

Situation	Anxiety (0–100)	Do the Opposite Action
1. *Ride down the escalator.*	*100*	*Look down without holding handrail, alone.*
2. *Stand on the subway platform, three feet away from the edge, looking down at the tracks.*	*90*	*Hands in pockets, away from other people, lean forward a little.*
3. *Stand on a balcony, one foot away from the railing, looking down.*	*80*	*Hands in pockets, alone, lean forward a little.*
4. *Stand in a stairwell, one foot from the edge of the step, looking down the stairs.*	*70*	*Hands in pockets, alone, lean forward a little.*
5. *Stand six steps up a ladder.*	*60*	*Look down, holding hands out.*
6. *Look down from the second floor of the parking garage, one foot away from the railing.*	*50*	*Hands in pockets, alone, lean forward a little.*
7. *Drive home from work on the freeway, on the section that dips down toward the valley.*	*40*	*Look far down the road, away from other cars, alone.*
8. *Look out the conference-room window on the twenty-fourth floor, one foot away from the window.*	*30*	*Hands in pockets, away from other people, lean forward a little.*
9. *Drive on surface streets in my neighborhood.*	*20*	*Alone, look from side to side, searching for areas where the shoulder of the road drops down.*
10. *Ride up the escalator.*	*10*	*Hands in pockets, away from other people, lean over the handrail a little.*

In chapter 1 ("Anxiety, Avoidance, and Anxiety Disorders"), you learned about anxious actions and identified the particular anxious actions that are a part of your anxious response. Review the list of your anxious actions (exercise 1.1) and keep it nearby as you build your own practice ladder (exercise 6.1). Convert any anxious actions that you might have an urge to do in the practice situation into opposite actions and write them next to each situation. Make copies of this worksheet so that you can use it for future situations or for developing several practice ladders dealing with different kinds of fears or anxieties. Remember, this is your stepping-toward-discomfort ladder, and it's your road map to overcoming your avoidance and fear, one step at a time. Knowing where you're going—where you'll start and end—takes much of the uncertainty out of your practice. Less uncertainty means less anxiety.

Exercise 6.1 Practice Ladder with Do the Opposite

In the "Situation" column, list a variety of situations and then rate in the "Anxiety" column how much anxiety you would feel (on a scale from 0 to 100) if you were to practice each one now. List the situations in order of difficulty, with the most difficult situations (those arousing the most anxiety) near the top and the least difficult situations (those evoking the least anxiety) near the bottom. In the "Do the Opposite Action" column, list your opposite action (rather than anxious action) so that you know to resist doing this anxious action when you practice stepping toward discomfort.

Practice Ladder with Do the Opposite

0	25	50	75	100
No fear or discomfort	Some fear or discomfort	Moderate fear or discomfort	Strong fear or discomfort	Extreme fear or discomfort

Situation	Anxiety (0–100)	Do the Opposite Action
1.		
2.		
3.		
4.		
5.		
6.		
7.		
8.		
9.		
10.		

HOW TO STEP TOWARD DISCOMFORT

Now that you've created your stepping-toward-discomfort ladder, you're ready to begin practicing each step of the ladder. To help you get the most out of every practice, keep the following steps in mind.

Warm Up

Before starting any of the following stepping-toward-discomfort (exposure) exercises, practice watching and waiting (review chapter 4). Over the next week—and before you practice any stepping-toward-discomfort exercise—for fifteen to twenty minutes per day, practice mindfully watching your anxious response. If you've forgotten the basics of watching and waiting, reread chapter 4 ("Watching and Waiting") before practicing. Before turning your awareness to your anxious response, begin with a few minutes of anchoring to your breath (chapter 4).

Close your eyes and notice your breath. Count your breaths or say to yourself, In, *then breathe in, and say to yourself* Relax, *then breathe out to help anchor your attention to your breath. If an anxious thought or image comes into your mind, notice it and wait for it to go away.*

Once you've practiced anchoring to your breath, let your attention open to include your anxious response. You're likely feeling a bit anxious as you anticipate stepping toward discomfort. This is natural and normal. In fact, you might discover that the worry you feel before an exposure exercise is the worst part. Once you step toward discomfort, you might notice your anxiety dropping a bit. Now, watch your anxious response without judging or analyzing it. Stay with that anxious response and watch what happens to it right now. Accept it, and remind yourself that it comes and goes.

Now you're ready to "FACE" your anxious response step by step.

FACE It

Select a place on your ladder to start. You might wish to start at the least threatening or uncomfortable step. Base your selection on not just your predicted anxiety level, but also your confidence (0 to 100 percent) that you can remain with your anxious response without doing any anxious actions, including distracting yourself, until your anxiety decreases. Later in this section, you'll learn more about this as you "FACE" your anxious response.

Face **your anxious response and watch it.** Over the years, you've fallen into a pattern or habit of turning away from your anxious response. You distract yourself from it. You try not to think about what makes you anxious. Distracting yourself means that you're not fully with your anxious response as it's happening. Distracting yourself gets in the way of your ability to learn that you can handle your anxious response in its full state, during the moments when you're feeling it. You avoid doing what makes you feel anxious too. When you must enter a situation that makes you anxious, you might have one foot in and one foot out. You might step toward discomfort with an eye to how you might escape the situation (for example, sitting in a theater but close to the exit). Learning to face your anxious response is essential to recovering from your excessive anxiety or anxiety disorder.

Anchor yourself in the present moment. When you step toward discomfort, don't step out of the present moment. Instead, watch your anxious response in the present moment and accept it (all parts of it) without judging it, analyzing it, or suppressing it. Anchoring yourself in the present moment means feeling what's happening now. Because you're rooted in the present, you worry less about your anxious response and learn more about it. From the present moment, you watch your anxiety rise, crest, and decrease rather than see what you fear about your anxious response: that it builds and builds without end. Anchoring yourself in the present moment will help you learn that you have nothing to fear from your anxious response. You'll discover that your anxious response is a small part of your experience that you can learn to manage and even value.

Check or resist your anxious actions. This means resisting all the subtle and not-so-subtle ways in which you avoid or lessen your anxious response. Do not say prayers or affirmations, space out or distract yourself, visualize positive outcomes, or do anything that takes you away from your anxious response. Instead, anchor yourself in the moment, using the skills you've learned. Rather than trying to avoid or lessen your anxious response, watch it and wait for it to lessen on its own. Anxious actions only get in the way of your ability to learn what's important for you to know. Checking locks repeatedly or calming yourself *during* an exposure gets in the way of true learning.

Endure your anxious response. Stay in the situation with your anxious response until your anxiety has decreased at least 50 percent or more from its highest point. For example, if your anxious response reaches 60 out of 100, then stay in the situation or with your discomfort until it reaches 30 or less. If you're having trouble enduring your anxious response and staying in the situation, drop down to a lower step on your ladder, or add some easier steps and start there. It's essential that you endure your anxious response until it decreases on its own, without any help from you—that is, without your using any anxious actions to lessen your anxiety. If that means starting at a slightly easier step on your ladder, then do that. It's better than escaping the situation or not staying in it long enough to get the full benefit.

Record It

Record the intensity of your anxious response using the 0-to-100 scale. Use the following worksheet to monitor your anxious response. Make several copies of this blank worksheet. You'll use it for all the stepping-toward-discomfort practices that you do. Use a copy each time you repeat a particular exposure, up to twenty times. If you are still quite anxious after twenty exposures, use another copy to track your progress for the next exposures. Enter the intensity of your anxious response before you begin the practice, at its peak or maximum, and at the end of your practice. Remember to stay in the situation or with your anxious response until your discomfort decreases to 50 percent or less of the maximum, or peak, of your distress. Tracking your anxious response in this way increases your willingness to try future practices, because you'll see that it's working.

Track Your Anxious Response

0	25	50	75	100
No fear or discomfort	Some fear or discomfort	Moderate fear or discomfort	Strong fear or discomfort	Extreme fear or discomfort

Beginning Level	Highest (Peak) Level	Ending Level	(Ending/Highest) x 100%
Example: *40*	*60*	*30*	*30 ÷ 60 × 100% = 50%*
1.			
2.			
3.			
4.			
5.			
6.			
7.			
8.			
9.			
10.			
11.			
12.			
13.			
14.			
15.			
16.			
17.			
18.			
19.			
20.			

Repeat It

Do it again. Repeat each step frequently. To benefit fully from stepping toward discomfort, practice repeatedly and frequently. Set aside thirty to forty minutes each day to practice at least three to four times a week. This is quite a commitment, but with consistent and adequate practice over several weeks, your life will open again as you reverse years of avoiding and fleeing from what makes you uncomfortable.

STEPPING TOWARD UNCOMFORTABLE SITUATIONS

You've learned a general approach to stepping toward discomfort that includes building a practice ladder and the procedure that will help you get the most out of every practice. In the next three sections, you'll learn how to apply this procedure in various ways. Typically, people with anxiety disorders avoid not only specific situations, such as driving on freeways, or specific objects, such as spiders, but also uncomfortable thoughts and images, as well as certain physical sensations that are all part of their particular anxious responses.

Stepping toward uncomfortable situations is a great place to begin your practice. You likely are more aware of the situations or objects that trigger your anxious response than the uncomfortable images or sensations that trigger it. Once you have created your situational practice ladder, go ahead and practice until you have mastered all the steps in that ladder. You might wish to create several situational practice ladders, depending on the areas of your life in which your anxious response is a problem. For example, Bart created practice ladders for both home and school, and later a ladder for public restrooms and restaurants. Breaking down the situations in this way helped Bart organize his practices and lessened his anxiety, because he had a plan that made the process feel more manageable. Remember to use the Track Your Anxious Response worksheet to monitor your anxious response.

STEPPING TOWARD UNCOMFORTABLE THOUGHTS AND IMAGES

Every day, we swim in a sea of thoughts, memories, and images that evoke a great many feelings. Certain thoughts and images make us anxious. This is normal and healthy. If you have excessive anxiety or an anxiety disorder, you likely have some images that make you somewhat anxious or uncomfortable. You might have noticed that you grow more anxious days or even weeks before you actually encounter a situation that makes you anxious. Usually, this means that even though you're not in the situation, you're imagining being in the situation. This image triggers your anxious response and intensifies the dread as the day nears in which you'll actually enter the feared situation.

For example, Roman began to worry and feel anxious each night as he imagined riding the escalator of the subway station. Although he lay safely in his bed at home, the image of the escalator loomed large in his anxious mind, and grew bigger and scarier each hour, causing him to toss and turn all night long.

As you practice stepping toward uncomfortable thoughts and images—rather than away from them—you'll begin to reverse your habit of avoiding any part of your anxious response, including certain thoughts and images. As you become comfortable with certain thoughts and images, you'll find that they enter your mind less often and, when they do, soon depart on their own, lost in the sea of other thoughts and images competing for your attention.

You'll use the same approach and strategies you learned earlier in this chapter, including building a practice ladder of images or thoughts that make you anxious. Often, stepping toward uncomfortable thoughts and images is a great way for you to warm up for real-life situational exposures. To create a stepping-toward-discomfort ladder for images, take your situational practice ladder and create a scenario for each step. For example, Roman developed a scenario in which he imagined standing on the edge of a step in a stairwell, looking down toward the landing below. In the scenario, he imagined feeling dizzy and light-headed as he struggled to stand on the edge of the stairwell. He imagined that his body was trembling and his knees were shaking as he tipped forward, feeling as if he were about to fall forward and down the stairs. He created an even scarier scene in which he imagined himself actually falling down the stairs: overcome with dizziness, unable to control his body, tipping forward, and tumbling down the stairs, one after another—powerless to stop. Roman created a ladder with six separate scenes from the least to most scary. Scenes lowest in discomfort included riding the escalator while feeling light-headed or driving on certain stretches of freeway, waiting for the dizziness to strike. Here's an example of one of Roman's visualization scenarios to give you an idea of how to do it.

I'm standing on the landing in the stairwell at work. I am stepping off the landing to the first step, when the dizziness hits me. I grab for the handrail but I'm so dizzy I can't seem to find it. I'm terrified, and I feel my legs and hands begin to tremble. I try to lean back from the edge, but the dizziness overwhelms me and I can't control my body. I feel myself tipping forward. I try desperately to lean away from the step, but I'm so confused that I lean forward instead. I begin to feel myself falling, and I am trying to stop but can't. I feel completely out of control as I fall. I'm in slow motion as I watch myself fall. I stretch my hands out to protect myself, but the fear paralyzes me. I can't move my arms as I slowly topple like a tree toward the steps below.

Try to include as much detail in the scene as possible and write it as if it's happening to you in the present. Write it in the first person, and include as many of your thoughts and feelings as you can. Also include the physical sensations that might scare you. In Roman's case, he included not only the dizziness, but also the trembling in his arms and legs and the sensations of tipping forward.

Make a Visualization Script

Once you've written a series of scenarios, you can record them and listen to them repeatedly. Try to record a scene that's no longer than one to three minutes.

Now, listen to the recording as you close your eyes and practice being fully with your anxious response. Do not distract yourself or do anything else to lessen your discomfort. If the recording is two minutes, listen to it three times, write down the peak anxiety level (using the 0-to-100 scale) for each practice, and then average these three peak levels and write this number on the Track Your Anxious Response worksheet.

STEPPING TOWARD UNCOMFORTABLE PHYSICAL SENSATIONS

Your anxious response consists of your anxious mind, your anxious actions, and your anxious body, which includes the physical sensations associated with your anxious response. For some people with anxiety disorders, the physical sensations are the scariest part of their anxious responses. For example, Roman, who has panic disorder, is terrified of the dizzy sensations he experiences in certain situations. The dizziness is a feature of Roman's anxious response, along with breathing heavily and sweating. For Roman to recover fully from his panic disorder, it's essential that he become less fearful of the physical sensations associated with his anxious response. This is true for people with other anxiety disorders too. If you're afraid of spiders, you might have observed that a photo of a spider can trigger your anxious response. Of course, a photo of a spider can't bite you and isn't dangerous, so what are you really trying to avoid? The answer is physical sensations associated with your anxious response (as well as scary images of a spider biting you). As you begin to accept and better tolerate these physical sensations, you'll discover that the urge to avoid the object or situations decreases, as does the urge to avoid the distressing physical sensations that arise as part of your anxious response.

In this section, you'll learn to approach, rather than avoid, the bodily sensations that are part of your anxious response. As in the other stepping-toward-discomfort exercises you've learned, you'll do this in steps. First, you'll do specific and *safe* physical activities to identify the physical sensations that are the most uncomfortable for you. Next, you'll create a ladder of the activities that trigger sensations closest to the physical sensations you fear. Last, you'll practice stepping toward discomfort by doing several of the exercises you've identified that trigger the uncomfortable or feared physical sensations.

Assess Your Physical Sensations

The goal of this assessment is to identify the physical sensations that are most similar to those that are part of your anxious response. Set aside about thirty minutes for the assessment. If you're reluctant to try this alone, invite your "coach" to watch from a distance. Try every activity on the list and continue doing it for the designated duration. At the end of each activity, list the physical sensations you noticed. There are several lines for each activity, in case you experience several physical sensations (for example, breathlessness, dizziness, and sweating). Then rate the intensity of the sensation on a scale from 0 to 100, where 0 is not at all intense and 100 is extremely intense. For example, if you felt breathless during one of the activities, you would rate the intensity of the sensation of breathlessness. Next, rate the similarity of the sensation to your anxious response. If you feel breathless when you're anxious, using a scale from 0 to 100, rate how similar the breathlessness you felt when doing the activity was to the breathlessness you feel when you're anxious. Last, rate the intensity of the discomfort, distress, or anxiety you felt about the sensation. Use the 0-to-100 scale again, where 0 means no discomfort and 100 means extreme discomfort. Look at Roman's assessment. This assessment was difficult for Roman, and he wasn't able to complete it without his wife watching from another room. He noticed that some activities didn't trigger any discomfort, whereas others triggered a great deal. Furthermore, Roman saw that dizziness was the primary physical sensation that frightened him and that the dizziness triggered by certain activities was identical to the physical sensations he felt in certain situations that he avoided.

Sample Exercise 6.3 Roman's Stepping toward Uncomfortable Physical Sensations Assessment

Practice each activity and, afterward, list in the "Sensation" column the physical sensations you noticed. Rate the "Intensity of Sensation" and "Similarity of Sensation" to the physical sensations that are part of your anxious response. Then in the "Intensity of Distress" column, rate how uncomfortable or anxious you felt about the physical sensation.

Not at all similar	Somewhat similar	Moderately similar	Strongly similar	Identical
0	25	50	75	100
No fear or discomfort/ intensity	Some fear or discomfort/ intensity	Moderate fear or discomfort/ intensity	Strong fear or discomfort/ intensity	Extreme fear or discomfort/ intensity

Activity	Sensation	Intensity of Sensation (0–100)	Similarity of Sensation (0–100%)	Intensity of Distress (0–100)
1. Shake your head from side to side for 30 seconds.	Dizzy	60	90	80
	Light-headed	50	70	60
2. Repeatedly (for 30 seconds), lower your head between your legs and then lift it quickly.	Dizzy	30	20	30
	Light-headed	30	20	30
3. Run in place for 60 seconds (check with your doctor first).	Heart beating fast	80	20	20
	Sweating	50	30	20
	Breathless	20	30	30
4. Run in place for 60 seconds while wearing a heavy jacket.	Heart beating fast	80	20	20
	Sweating	50	30	20
	Breathless	20	30	30
5. Hold your breath for 60 seconds or as long as you can.	Light-headed	10	20	20

6. While seated in a swivel chair (not while standing), spin for 60 seconds.	*Dizzy*	*90*	*100*	*90*
	Light-headed	*70*	*80*	*90*
	Nauseous	*40*	*50*	*30*
7. Tense major muscles, particularly your abdomen, fists, forearms, and shoulders, for 60 seconds or as long as you can.	*Muscles tingle*	*20*	*10*	*0*
8. Breathe very rapidly for up to 60 seconds.	*Sweating*	*60*	*40*	*30*
	Dizzy	*80*	*80*	*80*
	Nauseous	*50*	*40*	*40*
9. Breathe through a narrow straw for 120 seconds.	*Breathless*	*60*	*30*	*20*
	Light-headed	*70*	*80*	*80*
	Feel suffocated	*60*	*30*	*70*
10. Stare at yourself in a mirror for 90 seconds.	*See spots*	*20*	*0*	*0*
11. Hunch your head down while frowning and tightening your jaw for 90 seconds.	*Neck aches*	*20*	*0*	*0*
12. Walk with a 10-pound weight held to your abdomen for 120 seconds.	*Breathless*	*20*	*0*	*0*
	Heavy hands and arms	*20*	*0*	*0*

Exercise 6.3 Stepping toward Uncomfortable Physical Sensations Assessment

Practice each activity and, afterward, list in the "Sensation" column the physical sensations you noticed. Rate the "Intensity of Sensation" and "Similarity of Sensation" to the physical sensations that are part of your anxious response. Then in the "Intensity of Distress" column, rate how distressed or anxious you feel about the physical sensation

Not at all similar	Somewhat similar	Moderately similar	Strongly similar	Identical
0	25	50	75	100
No fear or discomfort/ intensity	Some fear or discomfort/ intensity	Moderate fear or discomfort/ intensity	Strong fear or discomfort/ intensity	Extreme fear or discomfort/ intensity

Activity	Sensation	Intensity of Sensation (0–100)	Similarity of Sensation (0–100%)	Intensity of Distress (0–100)
1. Shake your head from side to side for 30 seconds.				
2. Repeatedly (for 30 seconds), lower your head between your legs and then lift it quickly.				
3. Run in place for 60 seconds (check with your doctor first).				
4. Run in place for 60 seconds while wearing a heavy jacket.				
5. Hold your breath for 60 seconds or as long as you can.				

6. While seated in a swivel chair (not while standing), spin for 60 seconds.				
7. Tense major muscles, particularly your abdomen, fists, forearms, and shoulders, for 60 seconds or as long as you can.				
8. Breathe very rapidly for up to 60 seconds.				
9. Breathe through a narrow straw for 120 seconds.				
10. Stare at yourself in a mirror for 90 seconds.				
11. Hunch your head down while frowning and tightening your jaw for 90 seconds.				
12. Walk with a 10-pound weight held to your abdomen for 120 seconds.				

Build Your Stepping toward Uncomfortable Physical Sensations Ladder

Now, it's time to build a ladder consisting of the uncomfortable physical sensations from your assessment form. Include only the activities that generated physical sensations that you rated as 40 percent or greater in similarity to the physical sensations that are part of your anxious response. For example, Roman rated the feelings of dizziness, light-headedness, nausea, and sweating as most similar to the physical sensations associated with his anxious response. Order the activities that you'll practice based on how much discomfort the physical sensations cause you (not on how similar the sensations are to the physical sensations that are part of your anxious response). On the first and lowest rung of the practice ladder, list the activity that triggers physical sensations that are the least uncomfortable or scary. On the next rung, list the activity that triggers physical sensations that are the next most uncomfortable or scary, and so on. Remember, arrange the activities according to discomfort or fear, not similarity of the sensations to the physical sensations that are part of your anxious response.

Practice Stepping toward Uncomfortable Physical Sensations

Now it's time to practice stepping toward uncomfortable physical sensations. These activities expose you to the physical sensations that frighten you so that you can practice accepting and tolerating the uncomfortable and sometimes-frightening sensations that are part of your anxious response. Start with the first activity you listed on your practice ladder. If you're reluctant to practice without your "coach" present, that's okay. Go ahead and practice the first few times with your coach. Eventually, however, practice the same activity without your coach to get the full benefit of the activity and to gain complete confidence that you can handle the discomfort and anxiety without anyone's help. Follow the general guidelines for practicing stepping toward discomfort that you learned earlier in this chapter. Remember to "FACE" these uncomfortable and frightening sensations in the same way that you learned to FACE uncomfortable images and situations. Rate your anxiety or discomfort, and write it in the Track Your Anxious Response worksheet. Continue to practice until your discomfort level for the activity is 20 or below for at least four consecutive practice sessions. After you have finished the first activity, move to the next higher activity on your practice ladder until none of the activities creates much discomfort or anxiety for you. There's no way to tell how many practices it will take to reach a distress level of 20 or below, but it's best to practice as many times as you can and without much time passing between practices. Rather than practicing six times every third day, try to practice three or four times every day. Experts call this *massed practice*, and it's more effective than spreading your practices over a week. When you're tired, stop, but don't stop in the middle of a practice. This just strengthens the old habit of escaping from your anxious response—the old habit that you're working so hard to break.

Deep and lasting change—the kind that transforms your life—begins with stepping toward, rather than away from, discomfort. As you've practiced stepping toward discomfort, you've likely learned that you can handle more discomfort than you thought you could. In fact, you're likely viewing your anxious response differently—with a cooler head. Perhaps you've learned, at a deep level, that your anxious response is neither overwhelming nor catastrophic, but has a beginning, a middle, and an end, and that you can handle all these parts and far more than you thought you could.

In the next chapter, you'll develop a plan to minimize your likelihood of slipping back into the same old anxious patterns of responding. You'll identify your particular early signs that you're slipping back into those old rigid patterns of thinking and acting that have trapped you inside your anxiety box. You'll then review the skills that have helped you the most to recover from your excessive anxiety or anxiety disorder. You'll also learn the features of a recovery attitude—an essential part of your plan to manage your anxiety disorder over time.

CHAPTER 7

Keeping Going

Now that you've decreased your anxiety and avoidance, it's time to develop a plan to keep the momentum of your recovery going. After all, your pattern of anxious thinking and acting didn't set in overnight. It took years of thinking and acting in the same anxious way for you to develop the anxious pattern that has limited your life and caused you to suffer. It makes sense that it'll take time to build a new pattern of thinking and acting that becomes second nature too.

In this chapter, you'll develop a plan to strengthen this new pattern of responding so that it becomes easier and easier to step out of your secondary anxious response, or the anxiety box, whenever you wish. This plan will also lessen the likelihood that you'll fall back into the old, rigid, anxious patterns that signal that your excessive anxiety or anxiety disorder is trying to make a comeback. First, you'll review the early warning signs that you're slipping back into your anxious patterns. Then, you'll develop a plan to keep going that includes practicing what you've learned as you've worked through this book. Last, you'll learn the features of a recovery attitude, which is an essential part of the plan to manage your anxiety over time.

IT SLIPS UP ON YOU, AND THEN YOU SLIP

Although you have worked hard and are now better able to step out of the anxiety box, it's unrealistic to expect that your old pattern of responding won't slip up on you. It will, and when it does, it's important that you step out of the anxiety box as soon as you realize you've stepped into it. As you've worked through this book, you've practiced just that. You'll be fine, so long as you don't spend too much time in the anxiety box. This is what flexible thinking and acting is all about. The less time you spend responding in the same old way, the less likely you are to fall back into the same old way of thinking and acting.

Remember, your secondary anxious response is an old habit. Like all habits, it will slip up on you if you're not paying attention and watching for those first signs. For this reason, it's essential to learn those first signs, because the sooner you know you've slipped into the pattern, the sooner you'll know to use the strategies you've learned to step out of it again.

First, what are your high-risk situations? *High-risk situations* are those in which you're most likely to fall back into your secondary anxious response. What situations make you anxious? What objects, activities, and situations worry you long before you encounter them? What's happening in a high-risk situation that makes you anxious? What situations or activities do you want to avoid or convince yourself it's okay to avoid just this once? For example, any public-speaking situation—even if it's just speaking a few words—is a high-risk situation for Rosey. Similarly, activities in which Rosey is interacting with certain people—such as her principal or others in authority, or people she respects and admires—are high-risk situations for her. What are your high-risk physical sensations and the situations linked to them? For example, dizziness is Roman's high-risk physical sensation, and many situations can trigger it in him. High places where Roman might look down and feel dizzy, such as on a stage or a ladder, are high-risk situations for him. Escalators, stairs, balconies, bridges, and even certain actions, such as turning his head or standing quickly, are high-risk situations for Roman, because they can trigger dizziness followed by panic.

In what ways do you avoid triggering your anxious response? Do you avoid going to certain places or seeing particular people because you know you'll feel anxious if you do? Do you try to keep your mind blank so that you're not aware of the thoughts and sensations that make you anxious? Do you avoid triggering certain physical sensations that make you anxious—for example, by not climbing stairs because your heart beats quickly? For example, Roman avoided taking the subway to work because he had to ride an escalator to get to and from the trains. Similarly, he avoided looking down whenever possible, because he feared feeling dizzy and panicky.

What do you do—what anxious actions do you take—after something has triggered your anxious response? Do you check locks repeatedly? Do you check your math repeatedly when balancing your checkbook because you're worried about making a mistake? Once you feel anxious, do you try to distract yourself by watching television, playing video games, or talking on the telephone? Do you overprepare for presentations, even when they aren't important? These anxious actions can take a great deal of time and energy, and they are part of your same old, rigid pattern of acting in certain ways when you're anxious. For example, Tyra constantly asked her boyfriend if they were okay in order to reassure herself that he wasn't going to dump her. Similarly, Tyra spent hours each month working and reworking her résumé, but never sent it out.

What goes through your mind when you're feeling anxious? What are your typical thinking traps? What do you tend to overfocus on? Do you live under the tyranny of "shoulds"? Do you jump to the worst conclusion? What are the typical worries that signal that you've fallen back into your anxious pattern? For example, Rosey knows that when she's convinced that people can see her blushing, she's fallen into her old anxious pattern of thinking. When Roman predicts that his dizziness will cause a panic attack, he knows he's slipped into that old pattern of anxious thinking again. Similarly, both Rosey and Roman know that when their anxious minds jump to the worst, they've slipped into the same old pattern of believing that they can't handle embarrassment.

Tyra spent a few minutes listing her signs that she's slipping into her anxious pattern.

Sample Exercise 7.1 Tyra's Signs of Slipping into the Anxious Pattern Worksheet

High-Risk Situations	
List the people, places, activities, and things that trigger your anxious response.	*Anything to do with teaching: newspaper articles, websites, and even children, because they remind me of school and becoming a teacher.*
	Any bad news in the newspaper or on TV.
	Anything to do with my health: a cough, a spot on my skin, an ache or pain.
Avoidance and Suppression	
List the ways in which you avoid triggering your anxious feelings. Do you stay home every night? Do you avoid certain people, places, or activities? Do you try to keep your mind blank?	*Avoid sending out my résumé.*
	Avoid calling about getting a teaching internship.
	Avoid asking the teachers I know for info about how I might get a teaching job.
	Avoid asking my current boss whether I can have some time off to finish my teaching certificate.

Anxious Actions	
List what you do once something has triggered your anxious feelings. Do you check things repeatedly because you're afraid you made a mistake? Do you try to distract yourself from your anxious mind by watching TV or listening to music? Do you overprepare for tests or presentations? Do you try to lessen your anxiety by thinking certain things and in certain ways?	*Ask my boyfriend over and over whether we're okay.* *Distract myself by watching TV.* *Keep reworking my résumé rather than sending it out.*
Anxious Mind	
List what you're thinking when you feel intensely anxious. What's going through your mind when you're worried? What "what ifs" make you anxious? What thoughts hook you into a cycle of overanalyzing, reassuring yourself, or debating with yourself?	*What if I never find a teaching job and have to work as a nanny forever?* *What if I can't hold a real job because I'm not smart enough?* *My boyfriend is fed up with my worrying; what if he dumps me?*

It's time for you to spend a few minutes listing your own signs. Remember, the better you are at recognizing the early signs of slipping back into your pattern of anxious thinking, the sooner you'll be able to use the strategies you've learned to pull yourself back out. Slipping into the pattern of anxious thinking and being able to pull yourself out again is what flexibility is all about.

Exercise 7.1 Signs of Slipping into the Anxious Pattern Worksheet

High-Risk Situations	
List the people, places, activities, and things that trigger your anxious response.	
Avoidance and Suppression	
List the ways in which you avoid triggering your anxious feelings. Do you stay home every night? Do you avoid certain people, places, or activities? Do you try to keep your mind blank?	
Anxious Actions	
List what you do once something has triggered your anxious feelings. Do you check things repeatedly because you're afraid you made a mistake? Do you try to distract yourself from your anxious mind by watching TV or listening to music? Do you overprepare for tests or presentations? Do you try to lessen your anxiety by thinking certain things and in certain ways?	
Anxious Mind	
List what you're thinking when you feel intensely anxious. What's going through your mind when you're worried? What "what ifs" make you anxious? What thoughts hook you into a cycle of overanalyzing, reassuring yourself, or debating with yourself?	

BEGIN WITH WHAT WORKED

Now that you know the first signs of slipping back into your anxious pattern, you can apply the strategies you've learned in this book to pull yourself out quickly. Maybe not every strategy you've learned has been helpful. Maybe some strategies work great, so you use them most of the times you feel anxious, while other strategies don't work as well for you, because they're not a good fit. The most effective strategies are the ones that you'll use. Perhaps you've also learned other strategies that help. If it helps you more easily step toward discomfort and remain in the situation until your anxious response lessens, it's a good strategy. Remember, your old anxious pattern (that results in anxious actions) includes the strategies you used to get away from your anxious mind and body. If you've learned other strategies that help you approach (rather than avoid) your anxious feelings and resist (rather than give in to) the urge to do an anxious action, it's likely that they will help your recovery.

Look at the following worksheet. Place a check mark by the strategies from this book that have worked best for you. Does anchoring yourself in the present moment help? Do you find that the strategies to unhook from the meaning of a thought help? Does knowing your typical thinking traps help you more easily step out of your anxious thinking pattern? Does stepping toward discomfort lessen the anxiety you feel about your anxious response or decrease the physical sensations associated with it? Does it help you to jump back from your worst conclusion or test your anxious prediction? The best way to maintain your recovery is to know what has worked for you. Next, you'll take what has worked and develop your practice plan.

Exercise 7.2 Begin with What Worked Worksheet

Warning Sign	Chapter	What Worked	✓
Avoidance When you're avoiding feeling anxious or the physical sensations that make you anxious.	Chapter 6, "Stepping toward Discomfort"	Step toward physical sensations that make you anxious.	
		Step toward situations that make you anxious.	
Anxious Actions When you have urges to engage in anxious actions or if you've already given in to an anxious action.	Chapter 6, "Stepping toward Discomfort"	Stop what you're doing and step toward physical sensations that make you anxious.	
		Stop what you're doing and step toward situations that make you anxious.	
Anxious Mind When you begin to worry and fall into the same old thinking traps. When you're judging your anxious mind or criticizing yourself for feeling what you feel. When you're predicting the worst or overfocusing on the same old catastrophe.	Chapter 5, "Thinking Inside and Outside the Anxiety Box"	Calculate the validity quotient.	
		Test the anxious prediction.	
		Step back for a second look.	
		Jump back from the worst.	
		Unhook from the meaning.	
		Label your anxious thought.	
		Take the long way around.	
		Count the "shoulds."	
		Balance the "should."	

DEVELOP A PRACTICE PLAN

In this section, you'll develop your practice plan. This practice plan will help you maintain your recovery over the long term. However, no matter how good the practice plan is, it won't help you keep going unless you use it. Showing up every day to practice your plan is important. In a sense, you're signing up to be your own therapist. To that end, it might help to schedule times to practice, just as if you were attending a meeting with a therapist. Make an appointment with yourself, and protect that appointment the way you would any other appointment. If you find yourself missing these important appointments, this might be a sign that you're slipping into your old pattern of anxious thinking and acting. Set aside time every week to review your progress and adjust your practice plan, particularly if new symptoms arise or you notice yourself falling into a new pattern of avoidance or anxious actions. When new anxious patterns arise, include them in your practice plan so that you can apply what you've learned to these new symptoms. Remember, the key to managing your anxiety disorder is to enhance the flexibility of your thoughts and actions, and your practice plan will help with that.

Practice the strategies you've learned. You've learned a variety of strategies to enhance the flexibility of your anxious mind. Include in your practice plan those strategies that have helped you the most, plus strategies that you would like to practice more because you know they'll also help with practice. It's important to practice these strategies even when you're not anxious, in the same way that you would practice your golf swing before actually striking the ball. Practicing a skill when you're less anxious also increases your confidence that you'll do it well when you're feeling very anxious. Furthermore, if you tend to distract yourself from your anxious thoughts and feelings or try to suppress them, you might actually sometimes feel anxious without even knowing it. Practicing these strategies according to a plan, rather than just when you feel anxious, might help you catch your anxious response before it builds to a level where practicing the strategies is more difficult because you're already anxious.

Practice stepping toward discomfort. Perhaps there's no more important part of your practice plan than looking for opportunities to step toward discomfort. Increasing your tolerance to anxiety through approaching, rather than retreating from, your anxious response is essential to maintaining your recovery. Look at your stepping-toward-discomfort worksheets you completed in chapter 6. Include in your practice plan the top third of each of your ladders, and practice at least two or three of them every day. You might wonder why repeating what you've already mastered would help advance your recovery. Actually, you'll notice that even the steps you've mastered in the ladders, steps that no longer made you anxious when you practiced them regularly, will feel a little harder when you try them again. Furthermore, you might feel more anxious stepping toward discomfort one day than you do the next, even when practicing the same activity. That's because day-to-day stress can make everything a little harder, including stepping toward discomfort. Remember, though, you'll get the most out of those practices that make you feel the most anxious. However, even when you don't feel particularly anxious when practicing one of the steps from your ladders, you're building a habit—the habit of approaching, rather than retreating from, your anxious response.

Prepare for new symptoms. Regardless of the progress you've made, you'll likely feel anxious and have urges to avoid again. You might even observe new anxiety symptoms; perhaps you're having urges to avoid situations that you never avoided in the past, or you're having urges to engage in new anxious actions. This is particularly true when you experience the ups and downs of everyday life, the day-to-day events that stress us. Moving to a new city, taking a new job, and losing a friend or loved one are examples of the stresses of life. When your stress increases, your anxiety symptoms will likely increase too, and at these times, you might observe a new symptom in your anxious response: a scary new image or thought, or perhaps a new anxious action. You don't need to worry about new symptoms, however, because they don't mean that you're in trouble. They don't necessarily mean you're losing ground to your anxiety disorder or slipping back into your rigid old pattern of anxious thinking and acting. At the same time, you don't want to ignore new symptoms. Instead, focus the strategies you've learned on these new symptoms. Even though they might look and feel a little different, they're a likely piece of the same old pattern of anxious thinking and acting, so the strategies you've learned can help with them too.

Take a few minutes to develop your practice plan. Remember to include all the pieces in your plan to keep going. Place a check mark in one of the following check boxes each time you practice the strategy. You might practice some strategies many times each day and others many times each week. If you practice a strategy five times each week, check five boxes and circle the phrase, "This Week." If you practice a strategy five times each day, check five boxes and circle the word, "Today." As part of your plan to keep going, look at the stepping-toward-discomfort worksheets that you completed in chapter 6. Include in your practice plan the top third of each of your ladders, and practice at least two or three of them every day. List the activities you'll practice (stepping toward uncomfortable situations, thoughts, images, or physical sensations) on the six activity lines. Keep your "My Plan to Keep Going" worksheet nearby so that you can see all those check marks that affirm your commitment to keeping your recovery on track.

My Practice Plan to Keep Going

Exercise 4.2: Mindfulness of Your Emotions	☐ ☐	Today/This Week
Exercise 4.3: Use Your Breath as an Anchor	☐ ☐	Today/This Week
Chapter 4, "Daily Activities as an Anchor" section	☐ ☐	Today/This Week
Chapter 4, "'And' Take a Moment to Watch and Wait" section	☐ ☐	Today/This Week
Exercise 5.3: Predictions Worksheet	☐ ☐	Today/This Week
Exercise 5.4: Calculate Your Validity Quotient	☐ ☐	Today/This Week
Exercise 5.5: View from the Balcony Worksheet	☐ ☐	Today/This Week
Exercise 5.6: "How I Coped in the Past"	☐ ☐	Today/This Week
Worksheet and exercise 5.7: Plan to Jump Back from the Worst	☐ ☐	Today/This Week
Exercise 5.8: Count the "Shoulds"	☐ ☐	Today/This Week
Exercise 5.9: Balance the "Should" Worksheet	☐ ☐	Today/This Week
Exercise 5.11: Label an Anxious Thought	☐ ☐	Today/This Week
Exercise 5.12: Take the Long Way around an Anxious Thought	☐ ☐	Today/This Week

Exercise 5.13: Identify Your Hot Intrusive Thought Worksheet	□ □	Today/This Week

Exercise 6, "Stepping toward Discomfort—Top Anxiety-Provoking Activities from Your Practice Ladders"

Activity 1: _____ _____ _____	□ □	Today/This Week
Activity 2: _____ _____ _____	□ □	Today/This Week
Activity 3: _____ _____ _____	□ □	Today/This Week
Activity 4: _____ _____ _____	□ □	Today/This Week
Activity 5: _____ _____ _____	□ □	Today/This Week
Activity 6: _____ _____ _____	□ □	Today/This Week

FEATURES OF A RECOVERY ATTITUDE

Like many things, attitude is 90 percent of success. The strategies in this book will help you recover from your anxiety problems or anxiety disorder. However, as important and helpful as these strategies are, the attitude with which you apply them is even more important. In a sense, by practicing these strategies, you've developed a new attitude toward your anxiety symptoms that is counter to the way you've been operating. As you've worked through this book, you've learned the value of tolerating, rather than avoiding, discomfort; of taking risks rather than playing it safe; and of observing your anxious response rather than judging both your anxious response and yourself for feeling what you feel. This is your recovery attitude—a new attitude that reopens your world and frees you from the dread and fear that have pulled you farther and farther away from the full and meaningful life you wish to live.

As important as this new attitude was in bringing you this far, it will help you to maintain your progress over the long term too. It's inevitable that no matter how far you've come in your recovery from excessive anxiety or an anxiety disorder, you'll slip back, at least some, into your old anxious patterns. This step back, in large measure, is because your recovery attitude erodes over time. You might find yourself saying, *I'll wash my hands quickly, just this one time* or *I know nothing bad will happen, but why take a chance?* As you give in a little to your anxiety disorder, you'll notice that it becomes harder to resist giving in a little more. You begin to slide back into your old anxious pattern, where it becomes harder to resist the urge to avoid or to engage in the anxious actions that are part of your secondary anxious response. With time, your will to resist wavers and then weakens. Before you know it, you're back where you started. To keep going, it's important to understand the essential features of a recovery attitude and practice it every day.

Give your anxious mind a break. A recovery attitude includes giving your anxious mind a break. It's important that you maintain a nonjudgmental stance to the inevitable ups and downs of your anxiety disorder. Don't beat yourself up because you're more anxious one day than the next. Resist criticizing yourself because you want to avoid something today that you did easily the day before. You have the knowledge and skills to manage your anxiety and recovery over time. But a judgmental stance to how you feel at a particular moment is certain to undermine your best efforts.

For example, if you awaken one day feeling a bit more anxious than the day before, view it as an opportunity to practice the strategies you've learned. Criticizing yourself for feeling anxious won't help you manage your anxiety or maintain your recovery. When you criticize yourself for feeling anxious, you erode your confidence. You might then begin to doubt whether you can tolerate your anxiety or resist the pull to avoid discomfort or engage in those anxious actions. As you begin to doubt yourself more, you might also begin to doubt that you can accomplish what you've set out to do. Slowly, your recovery unravels as you become demoralized and lose your willingness to practice what you've learned. You've learned to watch and wait (chapter 4) in a nonjudgmental and present-focused way as your anxious response comes and goes. Watching and waiting in this way will keep your recovery on track.

Accept uncertainty. People with anxiety disorders like to be certain. They check the locks because they aren't certain they locked them, even though they checked them just a minute ago. They wash their hands because they aren't certain they washed off the last trace of dirt or germs. They avoid starting something until they're certain they'll have the time to complete it or do it right. In other words, they constantly search for ways to transform the land of "maybe" into the land of "certainty," because if they're certain, they know that they'll feel less anxious. However, certainty is a myth—a comforting myth, but a myth nonetheless. A recovery attitude accepts that certainty is impossible and that the need for certainty creates more problems than it solves. Acceptance or tolerance of uncertainty is an important feature of an effective recovery attitude.

Approach, rather than avoid, discomfort. As you've worked through this book, you've learned the value of approaching, rather than avoiding, what makes you uncomfortable. Approaching discomfort is an essential feature of any plan to recover from an anxiety disorder. In many ways, approaching, rather than avoiding, what makes you uncomfortable is counterintuitive. Our inclination is to avoid what feels uncomfortable, and most of the time, this works just fine, unless we operate this way "most of the time." Over time and with practice, you'll learn the value and power of operating in a counterintuitive way when it comes to your secondary anxious response. As you practice stepping toward discomfort (chapter 6), you'll sit with discomfort and wait for it to pass, rather than escape from it by either leaving the situation or engaging in some anxious action. Those who maintain their recovery over the years have made approach, rather than avoidance, the magnetic north pole that directs the compass of their recovery.

Do the opposite and perhaps a little more. Doing the opposite (and perhaps a little more) is the rallying call for those who wish to maintain their recovery over a lifetime. Doing the opposite (Linehan 1993; Allen, McHugh, and Barlow 2008; Moses and Barlow 2006) when you feel anxious is about turning toward and approaching the thing from which you usually step away. Doing a little more means doing the opposite but also looking for opportunities to act in a way that might make you a little more anxious. For example, if you have social anxiety disorder, doing the opposite (and perhaps a little more) means accepting an invitation to lunch, but then seeking out a colleague to ask to lunch yourself. Doing the opposite (and perhaps a little more) means that you're always looking for opportunities to bend that rigid pattern of anxious actions. You're looking for opportunities to not only do the opposite of what you've done in the past, but also try things you've never tried before—stretching the anxious pattern and stretching your wings in the process.

Seek support, not reassurance. Recovery from excessive anxiety or an anxiety disorder includes support but not reassurance. Over the years, you likely have confused support with reassurance, as have those who care about you and want to help. Seeking *support* means asking others to support your recovery plan and attitude. Seeking *reassurance*, on the other hand, means asking others to help you escape anxiety or discomfort. Seeking reassurance might give you some quick relief, but it won't last. In a few hours or days, you'll ask others again to reassure you. Support is essential to your recovery; reassurance is not. Furthermore, the people who support you, rather than reassure you, know that they're giving you something that's sustainable and, ultimately, in your best interest.

Practice every day. Finally, a recovery attitude includes daily practice. As you've worked through this book, you have mastered a number of steps on your stepping-toward-discomfort ladder (chapter 6). You might no longer find these steps very distressing. You might be comfortable with situations and sensations that once made you anxious. Congratulations! However, over time, what was once easy might become a little more difficult. To stay in tip-top shape and maintain your resiliency in the face of anxiety and discomfort, practice stepping toward discomfort every day. In particular, practice stepping toward discomfort for those situations at the top of your ladder (or that evoke the highest level of anxiety).

Although you might feel less anxious and avoid fewer situations today, over time, you can slowly lose these hard-won gains if you don't have a plan to keep your recovery going. Your plan to keep going includes the strategies that have helped and the willingness to practice them every day. *Strategies* enhance your *willingness* to step toward discomfort, and *willingness* is essential to maintaining your recovery over the years. In fact, willingness is likely the most important feature of your new attitude—an attitude that will guide you toward a fuller and more meaningful life.

In the next chapter, you'll learn something about the typical medications prescribed for anxiety disorders. If you're considering starting medications as part of your plan to recover from excessive anxiety or an anxiety disorder, you'll learn the advantages and disadvantages of these medications so that you can make the right choice for yourself.

CHAPTER 8

Medications for Anxiety

I f you have an anxiety disorder, you may be taking medication now, have tried medication in the past, or have discussed with your physician, family, or friends the possibility of taking medication. For many people, medication plays a short-term or long-term role in recovery from excessive anxiety or an anxiety disorder. Other people overcome their anxiety problems using the strategies in this book, without ever starting medication. In this chapter, you'll learn something about the typical medications prescribed for anxiety disorders, as well as the pros and cons of these medications, so that you can decide whether to add (or continue) these medications as part of your plan to recover from excessive anxiety or an anxiety disorder.

COMMON MEDICATIONS FOR ANXIETY

Physicians (for example, psychiatrists, family-practice doctors, internists, or other specialty physicians), and even nurse practitioners in many states, typically prescribe medications for anxiety disorders. Medications are generally safe and effective, and physicians often prescribe them in conjunction with psychotherapy. Your physician may prescribe antianxiety medications for the short-term or long-term treatment of your anxiety disorder, depending on your particular circumstances. Physicians commonly prescribe two broad classes of medications for anxiety disorders: antidepressants and benzodiazepines.

Antidepressant Medications

Physicians often prescribe three types of antidepressant medications for anxiety disorders:

Serotonin specific reuptake inhibitors (SSRIs). SSRIs block the reabsorption, or reuptake, of serotonin at synapses (spaces between nerve cells) in the brain. As the serotonin concentration increases in the synapses, you experience a decrease in the range of your anxious response. Fluoxetine (Prozac), fluvoxamine (Luvox), paroxetine (Paxil), and sertraline (Zoloft) are types of SSRI antidepressant medications.

Serotonin-norepinephrine reuptake inhibitors (SNRIs). Another class of antidepressant medication, SNRIs increase the level of serotonin and another neurotransmitter, norepinephrine, by blocking the reabsorption of both these chemicals at the synapses in the brain. Nefazodone (Serzone) and venlafaxine (Effexor) are common SNRI antidepressant medications.

Typically, these two types of antidepressant medications are the first that a physician will prescribe for long-term relief from an anxiety disorder. These medications are effective in the treatment of all anxiety disorders; they all produce about the same response and are generally safe for most people. Typical doses for the treatment of panic and anxiety are 75 to 150 milligrams of Luvox, 20 to 40 milligrams of Paxil, 20 to 40 milligrams of Prozac, and 100 to 200 milligrams of Zoloft.

Generally, people tolerate the SSRI and SNRI medications quite well. SSRIs and SNRIs have fewer side effects than other antidepressant medications, although some people still experience headaches, upset stomach, and sexual difficulties. These side effects are generally harmless and disappear in a few weeks. Additionally, some people may notice that their anxiety increases when they first start these medications. But the increase in anxiety is small when you begin at a low dose (such as 5 milligrams of Prozac), and it usually lessens after the first week on that dose. The physician then slowly increases the dose of the medication to a therapeutic level. It usually takes several weeks to begin to feel the full benefit of the medication. Sticking with the medication through these first few weeks is difficult, because this is also when the side effects are the strongest. This is particularly true if you experience an increase in your anxiety or panic symptoms. This, in itself, may cause you to want to stop the medication before you've reached a dose that will help you. However, side effects don't mean that something's wrong with your body or that the medication is harming you. Instead, the side effects indicate that the medication is beginning to work. Furthermore, although these side effects may feel similar to your symptoms of anxiety and panic, they're not really anxiety and panic. These feelings indicate that your body is adjusting to the medication, and if you stick with the medication for one or two weeks, these symptoms, as well as other side effects, will lessen, and you'll begin to feel less anxious in general as the medication begins to work. Your physician will describe these and other side effects to you. If side effects persist, your physician may switch you to another medication or add a second medication to the first one to lessen the side effects you're experiencing.

Tricyclic antidepressants (TCAs). These medications include amitriptyline (Elavil), clomipramine (Anafranil), desipramine (Norpramin), imipramine (Tofranil), and nortriptyline (Pamelor). In the past, physicians commonly prescribed these medications, particularly Tofranil, for anxiety and panic. Today, physicians no longer consider the TCAs as a first-line treatment for anxiety disorders, relying instead on the SSRI medications. Typical doses of TCAs for the treatment of anxiety disorders are 150 to 300 milligrams, except Anafranil (25 to 250 milligrams) and Pamelor (75 to 150 milligrams).

Although TCAs are effective in treating anxiety disorders, most people experience more side effects on these medications than on SSRI or SNRI medications. Some of the most common side effects are dry mouth, constipation, blurred vision, weight gain, and light-headedness. These side effects, as with SSRIs and SNRIs, are generally harmless and disappear in a few weeks. Additionally, as with SSRIs and SNRIs, TCAs may increase your anxiety a little when you first start the medication. Your physician can ease this initial increase in anxiety by starting you at a low dose (perhaps 10 milligrams of Tofranil). This initial increase in anxiety, as well as other side effects of the medication, lessens in a few weeks.

Benzodiazepine Medications

Physicians typically prescribe this class of medications for the short-term management of anxiety and panic symptoms. There are two types of benzodiazepines: low potency and high potency. In the past, physicians prescribed *low-potency benzodiazepine* medications, or minor tranquilizers, such as chlordiazepoxide (Librium) and diazepam (Valium) for anxiety and panic. However, physicians seldom prescribe these medications now, because most people must take these medications at a very high dosage every day to decrease the frequency and intensity of their panic attacks. Additionally, over time, many people find that they must take higher and higher doses of these medications to have the same effect on their anxiety and panic symptoms. This is why physicians prescribe these medications, and other benzodiazepine medications, only for the short-term treatment of an anxiety disorder. With long-term use of these medications, you may become psychologically and physically dependent, which makes it quite difficult to stop using the medication when you wish. At high doses of these low-potency benzodiazepine medications, you may feel very sedated or sleepy, making it difficult for you to function effectively at work, school, or home. Other common side effects are dizziness and problems with memory and coordination.

Physicians typically now rely on *high-potency benzodiazepine* medications for the short-term treatment of anxiety and panic symptoms. The most typically prescribed high-potency benzodiazepines are alprazolam (Xanax) and clonazepam (Klonopin). This class of benzodiazepine medication provides a stronger effect at a lower dose than the low-potency benzodiazepine medications do. For example, 1 milligram of Xanax provides the same benefit as 10 milligrams of Valium. Furthermore, people experience less sedation or sleepiness on these medications, and the medications work very quickly, usually within twenty minutes of taking them. The typical dose for the treatment of anxiety and panic symptoms is 1 to 4 milligrams per day, but if your anxiety is severe, your physician may prescribe more than 4 milligrams per day. Side effects of high-potency benzodiazepine medications also include sleepiness, poor coordination, and memory problems. However, the sleepiness usually decreases as you adapt to the medication, and your physician can lessen these side effects by starting you at a low dose and then gradually increasing the dose. Benzodiazepine medications appear to work by increasing the concentration of GABA (gamma-aminobutyric acid), a chemical in the brain. GABA dampens the firing of nerve cells in areas of the brain associated with anxiety. It's like a chemical "braking" system on your anxious response. Although this chemical brake works, if you take these medications for a long time, you can become quite sensitive to even the slightest release of the brake. In a way, people lose their tolerance to their anxious responses and are more likely to experience excessive anxiety and panic symptoms again when they stop the medication.

People who stop benzodiazepine medications typically experience withdrawal symptoms such as anxiety, difficulty concentrating, irritability, jitteriness, stomach upset, headaches, and sensitivity to light and sound. Although high-potency benzodiazepine medications all work quickly, they differ in the length of time in which they remain active in your body. For example, Klonopin has a longer half-life (the time it takes your body to eliminate half the dose of the medication) than does Xanax. The longer the half-life of the medication, the less frequently you must take it. The half-life of Klonopin is 15 to 50 hours, and that of Xanax is about half of that (12 to 15 hours). Therefore, people who take benzodiazepine medications with a shorter half-life may notice that their anxiety increases a bit when the concentration of medication in the body is low, such as when they awaken in the morning.

MEDICATION: YES OR NO?

Deciding whether or not to take medications for your excessive anxiety or anxiety disorder is a personal decision. You should make that decision based on a careful discussion of the pros and cons with someone knowledgeable and experienced in prescribing medications for anxiety disorders. Medications don't help everyone, but most people with anxiety disorders experience some improvement. There are particular times when medication might make sense for you. For example, if you're anxious and also severely depressed, and you can't imagine going through another day feeling the way you do, including a medication in your recovery plan might be the right choice for you. Similarly, if you have other conditions, such as attention deficit/hyperactivity disorder (ADHD), a medication for that condition can help you focus and make better use of the strategies in this book.

If you're in psychotherapy for your excessive anxiety or anxiety disorder—and perhaps working through this book with your therapist—and you're not making the progress you would like, medications might help. Similarly, if you're feeling frustrated because, in your therapy, you feel as if you take one step forward and two steps back, medications may help you make consistent progress toward recovery from your excessive anxiety or anxiety disorder. If the prospect of trying some of the strategies in this book, particularly those in chapter 6 ("Stepping toward Discomfort"), seem too scary and overwhelming, medications might help you take that first important step. Similarly, antidepressant medications also might be worth a try if you're practicing stepping toward discomfort and even the smallest steps seem too difficult.

For some people, medications can be effective at the right dose for the short-term treatment of anxiety and panic. However, many medications lose their effectiveness over time if you don't learn and practice other ways to manage your anxiety. When you practice them, the strategies in this book can help you manage your anxiety so that you can live without medication or with the lowest dose of medication as you and your physician think is necessary.

In the next and final chapter, you'll learn the important role that healthy habits—such as regular exercise, good nutrition, and adequate sleep—play in your recovery from your excessive anxiety or anxiety disorder. You'll learn the role that excessive caffeine and sugar play in aggravating your anxious response, as well as guidelines for improving your nutrition, exercise, and sleep.

CHAPTER 9

Healthy Habits

Many people with excessive anxiety and anxiety disorders develop unhealthy habits that cause them to feel even more anxious, as well as less confident and unhappier with themselves. For some people, their unhealthy habits—little exercise, irregular sleep, eating on the run—were in play long before they developed the anxiety disorder and may have been one of the reasons why their anxiety got out of hand in the first place. For other people, their unhealthy habits started after their anxiety problems developed. They skipped exercise because they were too worried and anxious to fit a brisk walk or a morning run into their day. They frequently ate on the run and grabbed fast food, or they ate foods high in fat and sugar when they felt anxious or down. They slept too little because they were anxious, and then they drank too much caffeine to keep going when they didn't get adequate sleep. Regardless of whether your unhealthy habits came before or after your anxiety issues, correcting these unhealthy habits is vital to your full recovery.

In this chapter, you'll learn about the important role that nutrition, exercise, and sleep play in managing your anxious response and in supporting your full recovery from your excessive anxiety or anxiety disorder. You'll learn about the benefits of regular exercise, the common roadblocks to starting and maintaining an exercise routine, and suggestions for overcoming them. You'll also learn how to develop a plan of regular exercise, plus how certain foods, such as caffeine, can intensify your anxious response. You'll learn about the role of nutrition in managing the ups and downs of your anxious response, plus simple guidelines to follow to make small changes to your nutrition. You'll also learn about the importance of adequate sleep—something that's not always easy to get when you have excessive anxiety or an anxiety disorder—and simple steps you can take that will improve the quality and quantity of your sleep.

HOW REGULAR EXERCISE, GOOD NUTRITION, AND ADEQUATE SLEEP CAN HELP

If you have excessive anxiety or an anxiety disorder, you may have trouble doing the things that you know can help. You may skip your exercise routine, because you're too worried about missing an important deadline if you take even thirty minutes to walk around the block. You may skip lunch or eat junk food at your desk, because you were too busy to pack a lunch in the morning. And what difference does it make? You don't remember what you ate anyway, because you weren't eating mindfully. You may stay up late because you're trying to fit one more thing into your day, and then lie awake worrying that you may not be your best at work the next day due to tiredness and short sleep. However, regular exercise, good nutrition, and adequate sleep are important parts of any plan to recover fully from excessive anxiety or an anxiety disorder.

With regular exercise, you'll better protect yourself against stress, and you'll experience fewer symptoms of excessive anxiety. Furthermore, not only can exercise help decrease the intensity of your anxious response over time, but also each time you exercise, you'll feel less anxious immediately after you exercise and for some time afterward. With good nutrition, you'll protect yourself from excessive fluctuations in your blood sugar level that can intensify your anxious response and worsen your mood. Through good nutrition, you'll also avoid substances that aggravate your anxious response, such as caffeine, and include in your diet substances that can calm your body and mind and even improve your sleep. With adequate sleep, you'll protect yourself from fluctuations in your anxious response and mood that happen when you're not well rested. You'll also guard against the added stress and worry that accompany poor sleep for many people when they begin to imagine and worry about the consequences of sleeping poorly.

GETTING AND STAYING IN SHAPE

Regular exercise is good for almost all of us, but if you have an anxiety disorder, it's particularly important. Numerous studies show that people who exercise regularly have fewer symptoms of anxiety and depression (Stephens 1988) and lower rates of anxiety disorders (Hassmén, Koivula, and Uutela 2000). Furthermore, exercise appears to protect people from developing anxiety and mood disorders (Kessler et al. 2005). There's another benefit to regular exercise. After you exercise, you'll immediately feel less anxious and experience a greater sense of well-being. In other words, while it may take weeks of exercise to feel less anxious in a big way, you'll feel less anxious for a bit immediately after you exercise, and you'll receive this benefit every time. In fact, the immediate effects of exercise on anxiety tend to be greater the higher your anxiety in general (Long and van Stavel 1995; Petruzzello et al. 1991).

How you exercise, and the amount and kind of exercise you select, will influence your willingness to do it. Here are some tips to help you build an exercise routine that you not only will enjoy but also, just as importantly, are willing to do regularly.

Get the right amount and right kind of exercise. If you exercise rarely or not at all, it's important to speak to your primary-care physician before beginning any exercise program. This is particularly true if you don't see your physician for an annual physical. Your physician may wish to conduct a physical exam and, depending on the findings, may even recommend that you complete an exercise stress test before beginning your exercise program. Although this may take time, it's worth it. Your physician can be a terrific source of information and support. Furthermore, you'll worry less about exercising when you know that your physician has given you the "okay" to begin.

It's important that you find the right amount and kind of exercise for you. It matters less what you do—whether you run, cycle, or lift weights—so long as you do it regularly. This means that it's important to find an exercise routine you enjoy. It's also important that the exercise routine you select give you the full benefit you want, without being so difficult and uncomfortable that you're reluctant to do it. In other words, it's important to find the right intensity of exercise.

The degree to which an activity influences your heart rate and breathing—from light to moderate to vigorous—is its intensity. To lessen your anxiety and improve your sense of well-being, you require only moderate-intensity aerobic exercise or a combination of moderate- and vigorous-intensity exercise. The US Department of Health and Human Services (Physical Activity Guidelines Advisory Committee 2008) recommends at least 150 minutes a week of moderate-intensity aerobic activity (brisk walking or swimming) or 75 minutes a week of vigorous-intensity aerobic exercise (running) spread throughout the week. Try for exercise sessions that are at least 10 minutes long.

The *talk test* is a simple way to monitor the intensity of your exercise routine. If you can talk but not sing during your exercise routine, you're doing moderate-intensity exercise. If you can say only a few words without pausing for a breath, you're doing vigorous-intensity exercise. If you don't feel winded at all, you may not be working hard enough. To get the full benefit from exercise to help with your anxiety and mood, try to stay in the moderate-intensity level.

If you're into accuracy, you might try using a heart-rate monitor rather than the talk test. Heart-rate monitors are relatively inexpensive devices that give you immediate feedback on the intensity of your exercise. Exercise intensity is gauged by your age-adjusted heart rate. For example, moderate-intensity exercise is between 64 and 76 percent of the age-adjusted maximum heart rate, and vigorous-intensity exercise is between 77 and 93 percent. If you're forty-one years old and you wish to stay in the lower end of the moderate-intensity range while jogging, you'd work to keep your heart rate at about 115 beats per minute. This is your *target heart rate*. Visit www.calculatorpro.com/calculator /target-heart-rate-calculator to calculate your target heart-rate range, or purchase a heart-rate monitor that will automatically calculate your target heart rate for you.

Fit exercise into your life, rather than fit your life into exercise. The best exercise is the one you'll do—regularly. In other words, people who exercise regularly have selected an exercise routine that works for them in their lives. For example, if you know that swimming would be great for you but working a visit to the pool (the drive there and back, the swim, the shower) into your schedule would be tough, swimming may not be the right exercise for you. As much as you think you "should" swim, it might make more sense for you to exercise in some other way. Perhaps it's easier just to walk out the door to stretch and run in your neighborhood, or you might bike to and from work. Of course, you can swim when you can work it into your schedule, but building your exercise routine around an activity that isn't practical may be a mistake. Furthermore, you may enjoy the activity less if you must deal with the stress of fitting your current life into a particular exercise routine.

Enjoy yourself. No matter how you choose to exercise, some days you'll enjoy it less than other days. If you run, one day you'll feel as if you're dragging a refrigerator down the sidewalk, and you must push yourself to finish the run. At other times, you'll have a glorious time. You'll run the same distance but feel lighter and faster, and you'll experience an enormous sense of well-being and joy that you can do this amazing thing. And running is an amazing thing—moving your arms and legs, keeping your balance, letting your body do what it's designed to do minute after minute after minute. However, even on those days when you don't particularly enjoy your exercise routine, you'll still benefit from the exercise itself; you'll feel less anxious immediately after you exercise and for days afterward. It can help to remember this as you drag that refrigerator behind you down the sidewalk.

You'll enjoy exercise more when you select a type of exercise you like: tennis, biking, or salsa dancing. Exercise doesn't mean running a mile or swimming fifty laps before work. Aerobic exercise can be fun when it matches your abilities and interests. This can include any physical activity you enjoy that gets your heart pumping. If you've never enjoyed exercise, you may wish to select three to five activities that you might like so that you can keep your exercise routine fresh and fun. Then decide when, in your daily schedule, you can commit to these activities. Be as realistic as possible. A thirty-minute hike in the woods after work when you must drive your child to tutoring and prepare a family dinner may be tough to fit into your day; shooting hoops in your yard with your child for thirty minutes after tutoring, but before dinner, might fit better into your schedule.

Reward yourself. The immediate benefits of exercise—less anxiety and a greater sense of well-being—are a great reward. Monitor your exercise routine (see the following log), including the decrease in your anxious response after you exercise, and use these immediate benefits to reward yourself. Additionally, you can monitor the pleasure of your exercise routine. If you have too many days of low pleasure, this is your signal to change exercise routines or use some of the strategies in the previous section to increase your pleasure when exercising.

Look for other ways to reward yourself when you exercise. Spend a few minutes enjoying a hot shower after exercising. Smile after exercising; say to yourself, *Good job*; and mean it. A good job is any effort. Remember, some days you'll feel great after exercising, and other days not so great. Reward yourself for the fact that you exercised rather than for the quality of the exercise. Try a dot-to-dot reward system. Using a piece of graph paper, draw or trace an image that represents a big reward. For example, cut out from a magazine a photo of the new phone you want or a palm tree to represent that weekend getaway. Place the cut-out image on the graph paper and trace lightly around it. Now, draw a dot at each point where the image touches a line on the graph paper. Each time you exercise, darken one of the dots and connect the previous darkened dot with the one you just darkened. Every third or fourth dot you darken, treat yourself to a small reward: a manicure, a movie, an hour to yourself doing exactly and only what you wish to do. When you have connected all the dots, treat yourself to the big reward.

Exercise to Decrease Anxious Response Log

0	2.5	5	7.5	10
None	Some	Moderate	Strong	Extreme

Month: _____ **Week No.:** _____

	Sun	Mon	Tue	Wed	Thur	Fri	Sat
Time of day							
Type of exercise							
Intensity (target heart rate)							
Duration (minutes)							
Pre-exercise stress/anxiety							
Post-exercise stress/anxiety							
Pleasure of exercise							

Develop an exercise habit. There are great things about habits, like the habit of saying "thank you" when someone does something nice for you or that of going to work in the morning even when you would rather go to the park. But habits can create problems too. Consider the anxious patterns or habits that are part of your anxious response. How helpful are those habits? Developing an exercise habit will help you alter the unhelpful habits and patterns that are part of your anxious response. A strong exercise habit can increase the flexibility of your thinking and actions, as well as your emotional responses to objects, activities, and situations. However, like many habits, they can be as difficult to build as they can be to break. To build an exercise habit, try to follow the four R's: *R*outine, *R*eward, *R*emind, and *R*elax.

The Four R's of Building an Exercise Habit	
Routine	Build an exercise routine that begins at the same time every day. Lay out your exercise clothes the night before. Wear them only when you're exercising so that you begin to think about exercise when you see the clothes (when washing, folding, or putting them out the night before).
Reward	Keep your exercise-monitoring log (see the previous exercise) nearby to remind you to exercise and to remind you of the immediate benefits of exercising. When you return from exercising, tell your partner or a family member so that this person can congratulate you. Set out a jar and place a dime in it every time you exercise, and then, when you have enough money, buy yourself a favorite cup of tea or a new song to listen to during exercise.
Remind	Make an appointment with yourself to exercise, and write "exercise" on your calendar. If you use an electronic calendar, create a reminder. Keep other exercise reminders, such as your exercise shoes or bag, in your field of vision. Ask someone to take a photo of you after you exercise (be sure to smile), and place it on the refrigerator, on the bathroom mirror, by your bed, or in another place where you will see it.
Relax	Wear exercise clothes that are comfortable and that make you feel good. For some people, that means wearing something crisp and colorful. For other people, that means wearing something loose, plain, and unassuming. If you will exercise in a gym, select a gym in which you feel comfortable and can relax and be yourself. Last, ease into your exercise routine. If you jog, spend the first few minutes at a relaxing and easy pace, and experience the joy of your body in motion. It's really an amazing thing!

YOU ARE WHAT YOU EAT—REALLY!

This section focuses on improving your eating habits to ensure that your mind and body function well, particularly when you're feeling stressed or anxious. Let's begin with foods that, if not managed, can cause a range of unpleasant reactions, including anxiety or panic. However, if you have significant concerns about your nutritional habits, if you have a medical condition that requires dietary modifications, or if you believe you're overweight or underweight, speak to your physician or a nutritionist about your concerns.

You might be surprised to know that certain foods and substances can aggravate your stress and anxiety. The two most common foods or substances you may consume regularly that can play a role in your ability to manage your anxious response are caffeine and sugar. While not all people are sensitive to these foods, if you are, you may know that foods like caffeine trigger physical reactions that feel much like the physical symptoms of anxiety or panic and certainly can make any anxious episode worse.

Caffeine

Of all the substances in food that can aggravate your anxious response, caffeine is at the top of the list, partly because we consume so many foods—and foods we like—that contain it. Caffeine can cause you to feel irritable and revved up, sometimes only minutes after consuming it. The physical symptoms that accompany that rush of excessive caffeine can feel similar to anxiety, which can trigger panic attacks. In fact, many people experienced their first panic attack after consuming too much caffeine for too long. Interestingly, even low doses of caffeine, such as from a chocolate bar or soda, can cause some people to feel shaky and experience increased heart rate and a rush of anxiety.

Caffeine directly stimulates your central nervous system and releases the neurotransmitter norepinephrine in your brain, causing you to feel alert, awake, and tense. Some people are quite sensitive to caffeine, and just a couple of sips of black tea can keep them awake all night. Other people seem to be impervious to the effects of caffeine. They can drink strong black coffee late at night and sleep like a baby. However, no matter how sensitive or insensitive you are to the effects of caffeine, consuming too much can cause you to feel chronically tense and anxious, which can aggravate your excessive anxiety or anxiety disorder, making you more vulnerable to panic attacks.

We are a caffeine nation, and many foods and drinks—not just coffee—contain caffeine. Teas, cola beverages, chocolate candy, and many over-the-counter medications contain caffeine. Unless you're sensitive to caffeine, limit your total consumption to under 100 milligrams per day. One cup of drip or percolated coffee per day would be about 100 milligrams. One cola or one cup of tea puts you halfway there. If you love your morning cup of coffee, it may be tough for you to omit it. However, even if you just cut back on your consumption, you may discover that you feel calmer and sleep better. If you're sensitive to it, you may wish to eliminate caffeine altogether, if you can.

If you love caffeine, it may be tough to change your habit. But if you're ready to try, it's best to take it in small steps. If you've been consuming large amounts of caffeine for a long time, you may experience symptoms of caffeine withdrawal—fatigue, depression, irritability, and headaches—unless you slowly decrease the amount that you consume. Start by calculating your daily caffeine consumption. Visit the Center for Science in the Public Interest website (cspinet.org/new/cafchart .htm) for the caffeine content of typical drinks and foods.

Once you have calculated your daily caffeine consumption, slowly decrease your intake over six to eight months. If you drink four cups of coffee per day, try reducing to three cups per day for a month and then two cups per day for a month until you reach your goal. You can substitute decaffeinated coffee for the cups you usually drink. Some people prefer this, because they experience pleasure in the coffee ritual as well as the coffee itself. If you're particularly sensitive to changes in your caffeine habit, you can go even slower. For example, if you drink three cups of coffee each day, you can dilute each cup by 25 percent with water, drink this for a month, and then dilute each cup by 50 percent with water, and so on until you reach your goal. Remember, people differ in their sensitivity to caffeine, so your final goal may differ from those of other people.

Sugar and Hypoglycemia

Although you can certainly consume too much sugar, your body and brain require glucose—a naturally occurring sugar—in order to function effectively. Much of the glucose we require comes from carbohydrates in our diet, such as bread, cereal, pasta potatoes, vegetables, and fruit. However, not all carbohydrates are equal. Complex carbohydrates, often called starches, are composed of a large number of sugar molecules linked together. Simple carbohydrates, such as sucrose, on the other hand, contain one or two sugar molecules. Refined white sugar, brown sugar, and honey contain sucrose and, for that reason, sucrose is a common sweetening ingredient in most sweets and desserts, such as candies and pastries. Sucrose breaks down very quickly into glucose. Starches break down more slowly into glucose than simple carbohydrates and therefore release glucose into the bloodstream more slowly. Complex carbohydrates are healthier for you because they don't raise your blood sugar rapidly, but instead release glucose into your bloodstream in a slowly and steady manner.

Although most people tolerate the sudden release of large amounts of glucose just fine, others are quite sensitive to its rise and fall in the bloodstream. People with hypoglycemia experience uncomfortable physical symptoms when there's a lower level of glucose in the bloodstream. They can experience clamminess or sweatiness, dizziness, weakness, and a racing heart. If you think these symptoms sound like anxiety, you're right. These are some of the same symptoms people report during a panic attack or an acute episode of anxiety. Hypoglycemia is rare and sometimes occurs in pregnant women, in people with high fevers or liver disease, or after consumption of certain foods or drugs. Although most common in people with diabetes mellitus, hypoglycemia can happen in people without diabetes, typically occurring several hours after a meal or first thing in the morning, when blood glucose levels are at their lowest. If you feel anxious and jittery a few hours after eating, in the middle of the night, or first thing in the morning, this could mean you're experiencing low blood sugar. When this happens, try eating a complex carbohydrate, such as a piece of fruit or a slice of bread to see if your symptoms go away. If you notice that eating decreases your symptoms or causes them to disappear altogether, and this appears to be a pattern, speak to your physician, who can order a test to determine whether you're hypoglycemic.

Developing Healthful Eating Habits

Scientists and experts on nutrition and weight have become increasingly concerned about the eating habits of North Americans. These experts believe unhealthy habits have contributed to a dramatic increase of obesity in both adults and youth (Singh, Kogan, and van Dyck 2010; Christakis and Fowler 2007). Furthermore, maintaining a healthful weight lowers not only your cardiac risk (Borodulin et al. 2005), but also your risk of diabetes (Chan et al. 1994).

In response, the federal government has created Dietary Guidelines for Americans (DGA) to promote health and reduce risk of illness (US Department of Agriculture and US Department of Health and Human Services 2010). The DGA recommend that we organize our eating habits around three important principles:

Eat balanced meals with few restrictions. To achieve the goal of eating balanced meals with few restrictions, consider the "rule of thirds" as a quick and easy guide. Include in each meal one-third protein (meat or beans), one-third fruits and vegetables, and one-third carbohydrates (grains and starch). Additionally, include some oils, fats, and sodium (which is present in many foods) in your meals, as well as key vitamins and minerals, such as vitamins A and C, iron, and calcium. If you're a teenager, include up to 1,300 milligrams of calcium daily, because most teens don't get as much calcium as their growing bodies require. Therefore, try to add some dairy into every meal and snack.

Perhaps the easiest way to develop healthy eating habits is to follow the Mediterranean diet, which includes vegetables, fruit, nuts, chicken, fish, olive oil, whole grains, and red wine. In this way, you focus not on eating less, but rather on eating more foods that are healthful. The Mediterranean diet is linked to lower rates of death, cardiovascular disease, cancers and cancer-related deaths, and neurodegenerative diseases (such as Alzheimer's disease and Parkinson's disease) (Sofi et al. 2010). The Mediterranean diet is also associated with lower likelihood of depression and anxiety disorders than a diet high in processed or fried foods, refined grains, sugary products, and beer (Sánchez-Villegas et al. 2009). However, although the benefits of the Mediterranean diet are clear, experts are less certain whether poor mood leads people to eat more unhealthy food or unhealthy food contributes to poorer mood. Regardless, a Mediterranean diet is a great way to feel better, grow fitter, and perhaps add years to your life. It doesn't hurt that the Mediterranean diet tastes good too. For additional guidance with meal planning and nutrition, speak with your physician or nutritionist.

Balance what you eat with what you do. Eat moderate portions, and get a moderate amount of physical activity daily. Your eating and activity level are out of balance when you eat large meals without being physically active. Similarly, limiting what you eat and exercising excessively is neither balanced nor healthy.

Regular exercise burns more calories but also builds muscle, and then having more muscle burns more calories. In fact, having bigger muscles burns more calories even when you're not exercising. As you progress with developing your exercise habit, you might notice a desire to eat more. If you're at a healthy and comfortable weight, follow your appetite and eat a bit more healthy food. If, however, you're overweight, you may wish to practice managing these urges using some of the strategies you've learned in this book (see chapter 4, "Watching and Waiting").

Additionally, you can decrease the frequency of food cravings by eating a balanced and varied diet without eliminating the kinds of foods you like. Furthermore, food cravings pass, usually within thirty seconds, if you start to do something else. When you feel the urge to open the refrigerator, stand and stretch, take a quick walk around the block, or start working on a more engaging project. Some people confuse food cravings with thirst, so drink ten glasses of water per day (particularly if you're exercising regularly), and grab a glass of water instead of food when you feel hungry.

Make smart food choices. It's not easy to make smart food choices these days. Television, radio, magazines, and newspapers bombard us with advertisements for convenience foods, the latest diet and exercise routine, and information and misinformation on nutrition and health. At times, it can be difficult to know what or whom to believe. Additionally, a busy schedule that keeps you away from home for most of the day can make it difficult for you to eat healthily.

You're more likely to make smart food choices when you have access to more healthful choices. For example, one brand-name chocolate wafer bar has 218 calories. Three part-skim mozzarella cheese sticks have 216 calories (72 calories each). If you're planning a snack, cheese sticks will provide you with far more nutrition than a chocolate bar, even though the calories are the same. Keep a bag of healthy snacks in a desk drawer, your purse or wallet, the glove box of your car, or your gym bag. Cheese sticks, nuts, raisins, and dried fruits are great, healthful food choices that are easy to find and will keep well in that desk drawer.

STRATEGIES FOR SLEEPING LONGER AND BETTER

Sleep—we all need it, and because you have excessive anxiety or an anxiety disorder, you may not get as much sleep as you would like. You may have trouble getting to sleep and staying asleep, partly because once you settle into bed and turn out the lights, there's nothing to distract you from your anxious mind and body. That's when worries and fears move in, causing you to toss and turn much of the night. If you then begin to worry about not sleeping or not sleeping well, you can bet you're in for a rough night.

About 30 percent of adults struggle with insomnia (difficulty sleeping) in some form at some point in their lives (Ford and Kamerow 1989). If you're a woman or an older adult, your risk for insomnia is higher, and for women, the risk of insomnia is higher at the onset of menses and menopause (Johnson et al. 2006). Approximately 40 percent of people with insomnia also have an anxiety or mood disorder (Ancoli-Israel and Roth 1999). You likely have noticed that when you sleep poorly, you feel more anxious and worried during the day. This cycle of anxiety, poor sleep, more anxiety, and even worse sleep is a vicious one that plays out in the lives of many people with anxiety disorders.

Most people benefit from seven to eight hours of sleep per night, and people get the most benefit when at least six of those hours are uninterrupted. Your body knows how to get the sleep it needs, and it will get the deepest and most important sleep first, in the early hours of the night, so that you can function adequately. However, a variety of medical problems can influence the quantity and quality of your sleep. If you snore or have trouble breathing during sleep (possible symptoms of sleep apnea), or you experience leg cramps or tingling, gastrointestinal discomfort, periodic leg movements, or chronic pain at night that stops you from sleeping well, speak with your physician or a sleep specialist. To learn more about sleep, check the National Sleep Foundation website at www .sleepfoundation.org for current information about sleep research and related topics.

Tips for a Better Night's Sleep

Many factors can make it difficult for you to get a good night's sleep. Some factors may be obvious, such as consuming too much caffeine or doing so too late in the day. Your sleep habits can influence the quantity and quality of your sleep too. Here are a few tips from sleep experts that can help you get a better night's sleep.

Allow sleep to come naturally. You don't "go to sleep." Sleep comes to you when you're ready. In other words, you don't control sleep and can't make yourself go to sleep, no matter how hard you try. Sleep happens automatically, and the best thing you can do is get out of its way. If you're anxious about sleep, getting out of the way might be very hard for you to do. Nonetheless, the most helpful attitude to have about sleep is to let it come to you when you're ready. Then what do you do while waiting for sleep to come? If you can't fall asleep within thirty minutes, don't fight it. Get out of bed and try a quiet activity, such as meditating, reading, knitting, or drawing. When you begin to feel drowsy, go back to bed. If you're still awake in another thirty minutes, try the same activity again. But no matter what you do while waiting for sleep to come, don't do it in order to get sleep to come!

Don't nap or catch up on weekends. That feeling of drowsiness during the day or near bedtime is *sleep pressure*: the pressure to sleep. Sleep pressure is the first sign that sleep is on its way. Sleep pressure is your friend, and nothing interferes with sleep pressure more than napping or trying to catch up with sleep on the weekends. Napping or catching up releases sleep pressure, which means you'll feel less pressure to sleep in the evening.

Eliminate or limit caffeine consumption. Caffeine and sleep don't mix. Excessive consumption of caffeinated beverages—such as coffee, tea, and sodas—and certain foods (for example, chocolate) and medicines can make it difficult to settle down when it's time to sleep. However, some people are more sensitive to caffeine than others are. You may be so sensitive that even one small cup of coffee in the morning can make it hard for you to settle down and sleep at bedtime. If you're having trouble with your sleep, don't drink any caffeinated beverages after noon. You may even wish to cut back on or eliminate caffeine in the morning altogether. In particular, don't use caffeine to give yourself a boost if you're feeling tired. Instead, take a five-minute walk around the block. Use a little exercise, rather than caffeine, to shake off drowsiness.

Exercise regularly. One of the best medicines for sleep is regular exercise. Vigorous exercise helps relax tense muscles and calm your anxious mind. Exercise can help release the day's frustrations and slow down your mind's tendency to revisit the details of your busy day. Twenty minutes or more of aerobic exercise at midday or in the late afternoon, before dinner, works best. Even a twenty-minute brisk walk in the early evening can help. However, avoid vigorous exercise within three hours of bedtime, as it can overstimulate your mind and body, making it difficult for sleep to come.

Take a hot bath before bedtime. Sleep tends to come as your core body temperature drops. The faster the drop in your core body temperature, the sooner sleep comes—all other things being equal. You can use this to your advantage by soaking in a hot bath just before bedtime to increase your core body temperature. A hot shower usually doesn't work as well as a hot bath, because it's difficult to get your core body temperature high enough during a shower. If you have a hot tub or Jacuzzi, you know firsthand how increasing your core body temperature can bring on sleep.

Set a consistent bedtime and wake time. Go to bed and get up at the same times each day, including weekends. Even if you're tired in the morning, get out of bed at the usual time and go to bed at the usual time. Keeping consistent wake and sleep times maintains adequate sleep pressure and prevents the tendency for your sleep and wake cycles to drift later and later in the day. Furthermore, your mind and body prefer a regular sleep and wake cycle, so try to honor this.

Create a quiet transition. Bedtime routines are a natural way to wind down and alert your mind that it's time for sleep to come. Beginning one to two hours before you go to sleep, turn off all electronic devices, because the ambient light from screens interferes with your brain's ability to slow down and prepare for sleep. Limit bedroom activities to sleep, and engage in all other "sleep stealers," such as watching television, working, and talking on the phone, to other areas of the home. Instead, read a book or magazine, listen to music, take a bath, or draw. Try eyes-closed exercises, such as meditation, mindfulness, or savoring. In savoring, think through the good things about your day and hold them in your mind. Savor the taste of the delicious green apple you had with lunch. Savor the sound of the ball when you made solid contact with it during your tennis game that day. Savor how good it felt to finish that project, or the sounds of the birds chirping on your walk to work that day. Savoring is a nice way to end your day and signal your body that it's time for sleep to come. However, no matter what you do—savoring, reading, or meditating—don't do it to get to sleep. That never works! Do it while *waiting* for sleep to come.

Transform your sleep environment. A comfortable sleep environment is another way to signal your body that it's time to sleep. Keep the temperature of your bedroom between 65 and 75 degrees Fahrenheit. Remember, sleep comes as our bodies begin to cool, so make certain your room is nice and cool. A hot and stuffy room can delay sleep. Install a lightproof shade or heavy curtains so that your room is dark, or wear an eye mask. Finally, use a fan to mask noises that might awaken you, or use earplugs.

Good nutrition, moderate exercise, and sufficient rest can increase your physical and mental energy and help you manage your anxious response over time. Although taking care of yourself in this way is unlikely to eliminate your excessive anxiety or cure your anxiety disorder, healthy habits are an important part of your recovery plan. Even small changes in your exercise routine can lessen the intensity and frequency of your anxious symptoms, enabling you to do things that you previously avoided. Furthermore, once you recover from your anxiety disorder, maintaining healthy habits will help keep you on track.

Conclusion

In this book, you've learned that anxiety and avoidance are natural features of an anxious response and that their sole purpose is to protect you. When you have excesssive anxiety or an anxiety disorder, the problem is not with your anxious response, but with the difficulty that you have in shifting out of this rigid pattern of responding to look around and see things as they really are. The skills and strategies you've learned will help you more easily break free from this pattern of anxious responding and, more importantly, will enhance your willingness to step toward discomfort: the key to breaking free from the wall of avoidance that has held you back over the years. As you use what you've learned to break these old patterns, your life will begin to open again, and I encourage you to fill it with the things that make life worth living: friends, fun, and adventure. I wish you every success in your recovery from your anxiety problems and in your journey toward a fuller and more meaningful life.

Resources

This section contains readings, websites, and other sources of information that might help you recover fully from your excessive anxiety or anxiety disorder. If you would like professional assistance with your recovery, you'll find websites in this section to help you find a cognitive behavioral therapist qualified to treat anxiety disorders.

ORGANIZATIONS

The following organizations provide information on anxiety disorders and list mental health professionals who treat them. The mission of many of these organizations is to promote the prevention, evidence-based treatment, and cure of anxiety and stress-related disorders through advocacy, education, training, and research.

Academy of Cognitive Therapy (www.academyofct.org): 1-267-350-7683, info@academyofct.org

Anxiety and Depression Association of America (ADAA) (www.adaa.org): 1-240-485-1001

Association for Behavioral and Cognitive Therapies (ABCT) (abct.org): 1-212-647-1890, clinical .dir@abct.org

Freedom from Fear (www.freedomfromfear.org): 1-718-351-1717, ext. 19; help@freedomfromfear .org

International OCD Foundation (ocfoundation.org): 1-617-973-5801, info@ocfoundation.org

Mental Health America (www.mentalhealthamerica.net): 1-703-684-7722 or 1-800-969-6642 (toll free), info@mentalhealthamerica.net

National Alliance on Mental Illness (NAMI) (nami.org): 1-703-524-7600

National Institute of Mental Health (NIMH) (www.nimh.nih.gov): 1-301-443-4513 or 1-866-615-6464 (toll-free), nimhinfo@nih.gov

READINGS ON MINDFULNESS, MEDITATION, AND COMPASSION

Brantley, J. 2003. *Calming Your Anxious Mind: How Mindfulness and Compassion Can Free You from Anxiety, Fear, and Panic.* Oakland, CA: New Harbinger Publications.

Dalai Lama XIV. 1999. *The Path to Tranquility: Daily Wisdom.* New York: Penguin Putnam.

Hayes, S. C., V. M. Follette, and M. M. Linehan, eds. 2004. *Mindfulness and Acceptance: Expanding the Cognitive-Behavioral Tradition.* New York: The Guilford Press.

Henderson, L. 2011. *The Compassionate-Mind Guide to Building Social Confidence: Using Compassion-Focused Therapy to Overcome Shyness and Social Anxiety.* Oakland, CA: New Harbinger Publications.

Kabat-Zinn, J. 1994. *Wherever You Go, There You Are: Mindfulness Meditation in Everyday Life.* New York: Hyperion.

———. 2005. *Guided Mindfulness Meditation.* CD set. Louisville, CO: Sounds True.

Kumar, S. M. 2009. *The Mindful Path through Worry and Rumination: Letting Go of Anxious and Depressive Thoughts.* Oakland, CA: New Harbinger Publications.

McKay, M., and C. Sutker. 2007. *Leave Your Mind Behind: The Everyday Practice of Finding Stillness amid Rushing Thoughts.* Oakland, CA: New Harbinger Publications.

NurrieStearns, M., and R. NurrieStearns. 2010. *Yoga for Anxiety: Meditations and Practices for Calming the Body and Mind.* Oakland, CA: New Harbinger Publications.

Somov, P. 2010. *Present Perfect: A Mindfulness Approach to Letting Go of Perfectionism and the Need for Control.* Oakland, CA: New Harbinger Publications.

Watt, M. C., and S. H. Stewart. 2008. *Overcoming the Fear of Fear: How to Reduce Anxiety Sensitivity.* Oakland, CA: New Harbinger Publications.

EXERCISE, NUTRITION, AND SLEEP

Books

Beck, J. S. 2007. *The Beck Diet Solution: Train Your Brain to Think Like a Thin Person*. Birmingham, AL: Oxmoor House.

Carney, C. E., and R. Manber. 2009. *Quiet Your Mind and Get to Sleep: Solutions to Insomnia for Those with Depression, Anxiety, or Chronic Pain*. Oakland, CA: New Harbinger Publications.

Dement, W. C., and C. Vaughan. 2000. *The Promise of Sleep: A Pioneer in Sleep Medicine Explores the Vital Connection between Health, Happiness, and a Good Night's Sleep*. New York: Dell.

Duyff, R. L. 2012. *American Dietetic Association Complete Food and Nutrition Guide*. 4th ed. Hoboken, NJ: John Wiley and Sons.

Epstein, L. J. 2007. *The Harvard Medical School Guide to a Good Night's Sleep*. With S. Mardon. New York: McGraw-Hill.

Hauri, P., and S. Linde. 1996. *No More Sleepless Nights*. Rev. ed. New York: Wiley.

Johnsgård, K. W. 2004. *Conquering Depression and Anxiety through Exercise*. Amherst, NY: Prometheus Books.

Krakow, B. 2002. *Insomnia Cures: Sleep Hygiene—Practice Makes Permanent*. Albuquerque, NM: New Sleepy Times.

———. 2007. *Sound Sleep, Sound Mind: 7 Keys to Sleeping through the Night*. Hoboken, NJ: John Wiley and Sons.

Otto, M. W., and J. A. J. Smits. 2011. *Exercise for Mood and Anxiety: Proven Strategies for Overcoming Depression and Enhancing Well-Being*. New York: Oxford University Press.

Silberman, S. A. 2008. *The Insomnia Workbook: A Comprehensive Guide to Getting the Sleep You Need*. Oakland, CA: New Harbinger Publications.

Willett, W. C., and P. J. Skerrett. 2005. *Eat, Drink, and Be Healthy: The Harvard Medical School Guide to Healthy Eating*. New York: Free Press.

Websites

American College of Sports Medicine (acsm.org): The American College of Sports Medicine promotes and integrates scientific research, education, and applications of sports medicine and exercise science to enhance fitness, health, and quality of life.

Diet Doctor (www.dietdoctor.com): This website provides information on exercise, health, and dieting. Also featured is a section on diet myths and accurate information on diets, including which method of dieting works. The website provides some information on exercise and workout programs too.

Fitness (fitness.gov): The website of the President's Council on Fitness, Sports, and Nutrition provides resources on fitness, as well as sports, nutrition, and general health.

Map My Run (www.mapmyrun.com): This website enables you to find a path in your community to walk, run, or bike. The site includes distances, maps, reviews, and ratings of the path and events in your community focused on exercise, fun, and activities.

National Health and Exercise Science Association (nhesa.org): The NHESA promotes healthy lifestyle choices and research into diet and exercise.

USA Fit (usafit.com): USA Fit is a program in which participants challenge themselves by running or walking in small but increasing amounts. After six months, many participants take and pass the final challenge, 26.2 miles of a marathon.

References

Allen, L. B., R. K. McHugh, and D. H. Barlow. 2008. "Emotional Disorders: A Unified Protocol." In *Clinical Handbook of Psychological Disorders: A Step-by-Step Treatment Manual*, 4th ed., edited by D. H. Barlow, 216–49. New York: The Guilford Press.

Ancoli-Israel, S., and T. Roth. 1999. "Characteristics of Insomnia in the United States: Results of the 1991 National Sleep Foundation Survey. I." *Sleep* 22 (Suppl. 2): S347–53.

Barlow, D. H., K. K. Ellard, C. P. Fairholme, T. J. Farchione, C. L. Boisseau, L. B. Allen, and J. T. Ehrenreich-May. 2011. *Unified Protocol for Transdiagnostic Treatment of Emotional Disorders*. New York: Oxford University Press.

Borodulin, K., T. Laatikainen, M. Lahti-Koski, T. A. Lakka, R. Laukkanen, S. Sarna, and P. Jousilahti. 2005. "Associations between Estimated Aerobic Fitness and Cardiovascular Risk Factors in Adults with Different Levels of Abdominal Obesity." *European Journal of Cardiovascular Prevention and Rehabilitation* 12 (2): 126–31.

Brown, T. A., and D. H. Barlow. 2009. "A Proposal for a Dimensional Classification System Based on the Shared Features of the DSM-IV Anxiety and Mood Disorders: Implications for Assessment and Treatment." *Psychological Assessment* 21(3): 256–71.

Brown, T. A., L. A. Campbell, C. L. Lehman, J. R. Grisham, and R. B. Mancill. 2001. "Current and Lifetime Comorbidity of the DSM-IV Anxiety and Mood Disorders in a Large Clinical Sample." *Journal of Abnormal Psychology* 110 (4): 585–99.

Burns, D. D. 1980. *Feeling Good: The New Mood Therapy*. New York: Avon Books.

Campbell-Sills, L., D. H. Barlow, T. A. Brown, and S. G. Hofmann. 2006. "Effects of Suppression and Acceptance on Emotional Responses of Individuals with Anxiety and Mood Disorders." *Behaviour Research and Therapy* 44 (9): 1251–63.

Chan, J. M., E. B. Rimm, G. A. Colditz, M. J. Stampfer, and W. C. Willett. 1994. "Obesity, Fat Distribution, and Weight Gain as Risk Factors for Clinical Diabetes in Men." *Diabetes Care* 17 (9): 961–69.

Christakis, N. A., and J. H. Fowler. 2007. "The Spread of Obesity in a Large Social Network over 32 Years." *New England Journal of Medicine* 357 (4): 370–79.

Eifert, G. H., and J. P. Forsyth. 2005. *Acceptance and Commitment Therapy for Anxiety Disorders: A Practitioner's Treatment Guide to Using Mindfulness, Acceptance, and Values-Based Behavior Change Strategies.* Oakland, CA: New Harbinger Publications.

Erickson, D. H. 2003. "Group Cognitive Behavioural Therapy for Heterogeneous Anxiety Disorders." *Cognitive Behaviour Therapy* 32 (4): 179–86.

Fairholme, C. P., C. L. Boisseau, K. K. Ellard, J. T. Ehrenreich, and D. H. Barlow. 2010. "Emotions, Emotion Regulation, and Psychological Treatment: A Unified Perspective." In *Emotion Regulation and Psychopathology: A Transdiagnostic Approach to Etiology and Treatment*, edited by A. M. Kring and D. M. Sloan, 283–309. New York: The Guilford Press.

Ford, D. E., and D. B. Kamerow. 1989. "Epidemiologic Study of Sleep Disturbances and Psychiatric Disorders: An Opportunity for Prevention?" *Journal of the American Medical Association* 262 (11): 1479–84.

Hassmén, P., N. Koivula, and A. Uutela. 2000. "Physical Exercise and Psychological Well-Being: A Population Study in Finland." *Preventive Medicine* 30 (1): 17–25.

Hayes, S. C. 2005. *Get Out of Your Mind and Into Your Life: The New Acceptance and Commitment Therapy.* With S. Smith. Oakland, CA: New Harbinger Publications.

Hayes, S. C., K. D. Strosahl, and K. G. Wilson. 1999. *Acceptance and Commitment Therapy: An Experiential Approach to Behavior Change.* New York: The Guilford Press.

Hofmann, S. G., and J. A. J. Smits. 2008. "Cognitive-Behavioral Therapy for Adult Anxiety Disorders: A Meta-Analysis of Randomized Placebo-Controlled Trials." *Journal of Clinical Psychiatry* 69 (4): 621–32.

Johnson, E. O., T. Roth, L. Schultz, and N. Breslau. 2006. "Epidemiology of DSM-IV Insomnia in Adolescence: Lifetime Prevalence, Chronicity, and an Emergent Gender Difference." *Pediatrics* 117 (2): E247–56.

Kessler, R. C., P. Berglund, O. Demler, R. Jin, K. R. Merikangas, and E. E. Walters. 2005. "Lifetime Prevalence and Age-of-Onset Distributions of DSM-IV Disorders in the National Comorbidity Survey Replication." *Archives of General Psychiatry* 62 (6): 593–602.

Linehan, M. M. 1993. *Cognitive-Behavioral Treatment of Borderline Personality Disorder.* New York: The Guilford Press.

Long, B. C., and R. van Stavel. 1995. "Effects of Exercise Training on Anxiety: A Meta-analysis." *Journal of Applied Sport Psychology* 7 (2): 167–89.

McEvoy, P. M., P. Nathan, and P. J. Norton. 2009. "Efficacy of Transdiagnostic Treatments: A Review of Published Outcome Studies and Future Research Directions." *Journal of Cognitive Psychotherapy* 23 (1): 27–40.

Moses, E. B., and D. H. Barlow. 2006. "A New Unified Treatment Approach for Emotional Disorders Based on Emotion Science." *Current Directions in Psychological Science* 15 (3): 146–50.

Norton, P. J. 2006. "Toward a Clinically-Oriented Model of Anxiety Disorders." *Cognitive Behaviour Therapy* 35 (2): 88–105.

Norton, P. J., and E. C. Price. 2007. "A Meta-Analytic Review of Adult Cognitive-Behavioral Treatment Outcome across the Anxiety Disorders." *Journal of Nervous and Mental Disease* 195 (6): 521–31.

Petruzzello, S. J., D. M. Landers, B. D. Hatfield, K. A. Kubitz, and W. Salazar. 1991. "A Meta-Analysis on the Anxiety-Reducing Effects of Acute and Chronic Exercise: Outcomes and Mechanisms." *Sports Medicine* 11 (3): 143–82.

Physical Activity Guidelines Advisory Committee. 2008. *Physical Activity Guidelines Advisory Committee Report 2008.* Washington, DC: US Department of Health and Human Services. http://www.health.gov/PAGUIDELINES/committeereport.aspx.

Regier, D. A., D. S. Rae, W. E. Narrow, C. T. Kaelber, and A. F. Schatzberg. 1998. "Prevalence of Anxiety Disorders and Their Comorbidity with Mood and Addictive Disorders." *British Journal of Psychiatry,* Vol 173(Suppl. 34), Jul 1998, 24–28.

Salters-Pedneault, K., M. T. Tull, and L. Roemer. 2004. "The Role of Avoidance of Emotional Material in the Anxiety Disorders." *Applied and Preventive Psychology* 11 (2): 95–114.

Sánchez-Villegas, A., M. Delgado-Rodriguez, A. Alonso, J. Schlatter, F. Lahortiga, L. Serra Majem, and M. A. Martínez-González. 2009. "Association of the Mediterranean Dietary Pattern with the Incidence of Depression: The Seguimiento Universidad de Navarra/University of Navarra Follow-Up (SUN) Cohort." *Archives of General Psychiatry* 66 (10): 1090–98.

Singh, G. K., M. D. Kogan, and P. C. van Dyck. 2010. "Changes in State-Specific Childhood Obesity and Overweight Prevalence in the United States from 2003 to 2007." *Archives of Pediatrics and Adolescent Medicine* 164 (7): 598–607.

Sofi, F., R. Abbate, G. F. Gensini, and A. Casini. 2010. "Accruing Evidence on Benefits of Adherence to the Mediterranean Diet on Health: An Updated Systematic Review and Meta-analysis." *American Journal of Clinical Nutrition* 92 (5): 1189–96.

Stephens, T. 1988. "Physical Activity and Mental Health in the United States and Canada: Evidence from Four Popular Surveys." *Preventive Medicine* 17 (1): 35–47.

Titchener, E. B. 1910. *A Text-Book of Psychology.* New York: The Macmillan Company.

US Department of Agriculture and US Department of Health and Human Services. 2010. *Dietary Guidelines for Americans, 2010.* 7th ed. Washington, DC: US Government Printing Office. http://www.cnpp.usda.gov/Publications/DietaryGuidelines/2010/PolicyDoc.pd.

Wegner, D. M. 1994. "Ironic Processes of Mental Control." *Psychological Review* 101 (1): 34–52.

Michael A. Tompkins, PhD, is a founding partner of the San Francisco Bay Area Center for Cognitive Therapy, diplomate of the Academy of Cognitive Therapy, and assistant clinical professor at the University of California, Berkeley. He is author of *OCD: A Guide for the Newly Diagnosed* and *Digging Out: Helping Your Loved One Manage Clutter, Hoarding, and Compulsive Acquiring.*

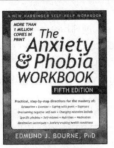

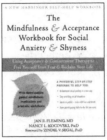

FROM OUR PUBLISHER—

As the publisher at New Harbinger and a clinical psychologist since 1978, I know that emotional problems are best helped with evidence-based therapies. These are the treatments derived from scientific research (randomized controlled trials) that show what works. Whether these treatments are delivered by trained clinicians or found in a self-help book, they are designed to provide you with proven strategies to overcome your problem.

Therapies that aren't evidence-based—whether offered by clinicians or in books—are much less likely to help. In fact, therapies that aren't guided by science may not help you at all. That's why this New Harbinger book is based on scientific evidence that the treatment can relieve emotional pain.

This is important: if this book isn't enough, and you need the help of a skilled therapist, use the following resources to find a clinician trained in the evidence-based protocols appropriate for your problem. And if you need more support—a community that understands what you're going through and can show you ways to cope—resources for that are provided below, as well.

Real help is available for the problems you have been struggling with. The skills you can learn from evidence-based therapies will change your life.

Matthew McKay, PhD
Publisher, New Harbinger Publications

new harbinger
CELEBRATING
40 YEARS

The following organizations can help you find a therapist:

The Association for Behavioral & Cognitive Therapies (ABCT) Find-a-Therapist service offers a list of therapists schooled in CBT techniques. Therapists listed are licensed professionals who have met the membership requirements of ABCT and who have chosen to appear in the directory.
Please visit www.abct.org and click on *Find a Therapist*.

Association for Contextual Behavioral Science (ACBS)
please visit www.contextualscience.org and click on *Find an ACT Therapist*.

For additional support for patients, family, and friends, please contact the following:

Anxiety and Depression Association of American (ADAA)
please visit www.adaa.org

National Alliance on Mental Illness (NAMI)
please visit www.nami.org